Praise for Daunting to DOable

Karen offers practical guidance and tips to make business development approachable by all. She brings together real-world examples and her professional expertise into a highly useful resource that truly will move objectives from daunting to doable.

Despina Kartson
Chief Business Development & Marketing Officer
Morgan, Lewis & Bockius LLP

Rainmaking may not always come naturally to lawyers, but through using the approach outlined in Daunting to DOable and working with Karen, we have seen that the skills can be taught. Often what holds lawyers back from actively developing business is feeling they simply don't have the time to focus on it. Karen gets lawyers. She really listens to each person's concerns and reservations, and works with them to shape her process and techniques to fit their reality and personality. Maybe most importantly, she shows them how to use these tools to build a gratifying legal career.

Ronald H. Shechtman
Managing Partner,
Pryor Cashman LLP

Daunting to DOable: You CAN Make IT Rain presents a highly practical approach to business development for lawyers that is based on deep experience and psychological insight. I've seen Karen's approach to business development in action, and it works.

Jamie Hutchinson
Chief Administrative Partner
Alston & Bird LLP

The word "relationship" pervades Daunting to DOable, and it should. That's the foundation of any professional service business. Karen's background as a psychologist is front-and-center in her advice on how to change your own behavior based on others' behavior to build the kind of real, lasting relationships that lead to business.

Geoff Goldberg
Chief Advancement Officer
McCarter & English

Karen really gets relationships and combines that with an amazing understanding of how to motivate attorneys. She's an excellent coach that drives real results! Daunting to DOable: You CAN Make It Rain should be a must read for all law firm attorneys focused on business development (and that should be all of them).

Lee R. Garfinkle
Senior Law Firm Marketing and Business Development Executive

Karen Kahn has many years of being a business development coach extraordinaire. In Daunting to DOable, she provides both basics and insights to those looking to build business. An easy read by a great coach. Get out the umbrella!

Cathy Fleming
Fleming Ruvoldt, PLLC
Former President, National Association of Women Lawyers

In Daunting to DOable: You Can Make It Rain, Karen Kahn has written a fantastic book that is timely and practical. In a hyper-competitive legal market that is experiencing modest growth, it is absolutely necessary that lawyers approach business development in a way that is effective and most comfortable for them (and their prospective clients). Dr. Kahn provides several useful tips that will help readers generate business by simply listening and offering assistance, and not by coming across as used car salesmen.

Kenneth O. C. Imo, Esq.
Director of Diversity
WilmerHale LLP

A sensible approach to building a law business, presented succinctly and with practical application. Karen "gets it." In Daunting to DOable she shines a light on the nagging doubts that inhibit business development and gently urges the reader beyond personal roadblocks. Her approach works, and it's not nearly as hard as trying to lose ten pounds!

Diane Ambler
Partner
K & L Gates, LLP

Karen Kahn's book is both insightful and witty. The book removes the mystery from business development and sets forth in unprecedented fashion the specific processes that foster successful rainmaking at law firms. Lawyers at all stages in their careers will benefit from the many wise and strategic tips in this book.

Senior Partner at an AmLaw 25 Firm

Karen has captured the critical concepts and pathway to success as a rainmaker in terms that are easily understood, implemented and repeated. A great easy read and a map to success.

Harold Ruvoldt
Partner
Sullivan Ruvoldt, PLLC

Daunting to DOable is a must-read for anyone wanting to learn clear steps for improving their business development skills. Karen's thoughtful advice and easy-to-understand method provide solid strategies for identifying your WHOs and developing your HOW plan of action. It also includes wonderful stories and insightful tips on how to handle the practical challenges of business development, including internal self-doubt. Karen's colorful anecdotes complement her methodology with clear evidence that her techniques work. Her book provides the recipe for successful business development in today's ever-changing legal marketplace.

Audra Dial
Atlanta Office Managing Partner
Kilpatrick Townsend & Stockton

Karen Kahn has developed a method for business development that will change the way you think and work. Her ideas are simple to implement and highly effective for anyone from novice marketer to established rainmaker. Karen's passion and energy shine through in this book. She is a brilliant coach, thought leader, and all-around terrific woman! Thank you for helping so many of us understand how to DO business development.

Angela Beranek Brandt
Partner, Larson King, LLP
and Officer of the National Association of Women Lawyers

Karen's psychological and coaching training shine through in her approach to business development and her recognition that authenticity is central to any relationship. If you are trying to figure out how to make your business truly You, Inc. in the sense that it feels comfortable and natural to you, Daunting to DOable is a must-read.

Katherine Larkin-Wong
President
Ms. JD

Karen Kahn is a pragmatic and passionate thought leader whose approach, laid out in Daunting to DOAble, provides measurable results. For lawyers who undertake the daunting task of upping their game, this book provides practical advice for picking the right strategy and getting it done.

Kit Chaskin
Partner, Director of Women's Initiative Network
Reed Smith

Karen Kahn's new book provides a fresh insight into the intersection between valuable relationships and business development. Filled with Karen's passion for impacting the growth and development of leaders, Daunting to DOable provides a clear roadmap designed to easily utilize and help readers thrive and authentically reach their desired business development goals.

Tanya Y. Johnson
Senior Diversity Manager
Perkins Coie LLP

Combine decades of psychological insights into human motivation and the fears that stop us, with outstanding coaching skills, add a pinch of encouragement, a teaspoon of love and a step-by-step plan of action and you have a recipe for success. In Daunting to DOable, Karen has translated years of experience, deep knowledge and a passionate desire to help others achieve their dreams into a road map for career and business development success that is highly consistent with your personal values and goals. The smartest move you will make this year is blocking out some time in your schedule to read this book and begin to implement its recommendations.

John "The Purple Coach" Mitchell
KM Advisors, LLC

As coach, psychologist, and gender expert, Daunting to DOable: You CAN Make it Rain brings to the table a powerful and blended perspective that all lawyers can learn from. By focusing on multiple approaches for the HOWs, Karen empowers the reader to partner with many resources to find a natural, individual approach to develop a sustainable and measurable process for rainmaking success.

Jeanne Cullen
Partner at an AmLaw 50 law firm

Daunting to DOable is a quick, easy, and fun read, but most importantly, the approach works. Karen challenged me to make big plans, set big goals, and to execute. In order to execute and reach my goals, I followed Karen's plan by listening, taking action, and believing in myself. In less than 12 months under Karen's plan, I achieved my goal of equity partnership. Simply, Karen helped me realize my goals were DOable, and if you follow her steps, yours will be too.

Leah Rudnicki
Partner
Reed Smith

Daunting
to
DOable

You CAN Make It Rain

KAREN B. KAHN, EdD, PCC

Includes special chapter on the Art and Science of Social Media
by Guy Alvarez

Daunting to DOable
You *CAN* Make It Rain
Karen B. Kahn, EdD, PCC

Briggs Publishing
Published by Briggs Publishing, Westport, Connecticut

Editor: Lauren Hidden, www.HiddenHelpers.com
Proofreader: Tahlia Day, www.katharosediting.com
Index: Elena Gwynne, www.quillandinkindexing.com
Cover and Interior design: Susan Heilig, www.ideadesign-dc.com

Library of Congress Control Number: 2015902095
ISBN: 978-0-9861100-0-9

ATTENTION CORPORATIONS, UNIVERSITIES, COLLEGES AND PROFESSIONAL ORGANIZATIONS: Quantity discounts are available on bulk purchases of this book for educational, gift purposes, or as premiums for increasing magazine subscriptions or renewals. Special books or book excerpts can also be created to fit specific needs. For information, please contact Briggs Publishing, 15 Danbury Avenue, Westport, CT 06880; phone: 512-250-8546

Dedicated to Marty Africa.
May her memory continue to inspire.

Table of Contents

Part III: Your HOWs Tool Box   47

Part IV: Tools, Systems, Processes   125

Acknowledgments

The desire to write this book percolated for a long time. And, as many of us tend to do, I procrastinated getting started. One day, while I was speaking to fabulous lawyer Andree St. Martin from Groom Law Group about her struggle to complete a project, she asked me if I ever had this challenge. In that moment, I shared my frustration with my failure to move forward with this book. Bonded by determination to move our goals forward, work on this book began. Therefore, I start this section of appreciation by thanking Andree for expecting from me what I encouraged in her.

Writing comes with many moments of doubt, blocks and discouragement. I am so very fortunate to have been befriended by some women lawyers who will answer the phone any time I call, give me honest advice and feedback and, in the spirit of Sally Field at the Academy Awards, "They really like me." Cathy Fleming, Kit Chaskin, Diane Ambler, Despina Kartson, Angela Brandt and Sylvia James—your support means more to me than I can express.

My partners and collaborants (yes, I made up that word and I am sticking to it!) at Threshold Advisors have consistently been there for me encouraging, praising and patient. When I let my leadership take a back seat to completing this book they shouted, "Go for it! No problem!" This means so much to me. Thank you, Andi Groomes, Marci Wilf and Andrew Ellowitt; also Andrew Cohn and Marty Maddin.

John Mitchell—thank you for all you did to transition me from the world of psychology to the community of law. Acknowledging your support and tutelage is an understatement. Your wisdom, friendship and role model as a leader continue to teach me a great deal.

To the National Association of Women Lawyers: Midyear 2013 is the first place I presented *Daunting to DOable*. Janet Stivens, you helped coin the title that has received so many compliments; thank you. Thank you, NAWL, for openly including me, a shrink, not a lawyer, in the vibrant community.

I love living in the world of relationships and connections where giving and helping is exchanged so freely. This has resulted in treasured relationships with many people. Sadly, I know I will forget some; please forgive me. As I write each name I am filled with memories and acknowledgement of fabulous conversations and mutuality: Joanna Horsnail, Sharon Bowen, Leah Sanzari, Lori Pines, Brenda Dieck, Lonie Hassle, Leah Rudnicki, Audra Dial, Dorian Denberg, Monica Parham, Lisa Horowitz, Lorraine Koc (your support propelled me into NAWL), Anna Lamie, Guy Alvarez, Andrew Sobel, Jamie Hutchinson and many others.

With enormous gratitude, I acknowledge Dr. Anne Robinson, who took a moment out of a college class to randomly say, "Karen, you have to become a psychologist." Thank you for pointing me in the right direction and setting the framework for embracing differences, confronting biases, and insisting that I never stop being attentive to my own "isms."

Thank you to Lauren Hidden for being my editor for so many years and training me to be alert to the "active voice."

Thank you to Susan Heilig for her friendship and her expertise in book design to help turn my words into the book you hold in your hands.

Janica Smith, my virtual assistant and book coach (virtual because she works in Austin and my office is in Connecticut—it works!), there is no end to my appreciation for the many, many things you do to keep me moving forward, and, because of your expertise in self-publishing, I am able to publish and share my ideas. Thank you for always being there.

Love keeps my heart beating. I am blessed with the most wonderful, supportive family whose belief in me never seems to waver, even when they don't totally understand what I do. My father, Edwin Kahn, is my connection to the law. While he died thirty years ago, his license to practice law, dated February 19, 1942, hangs in my office, quietly offering me legitimacy to work with his colleagues. My brother, Dan Kahn, and sister, Shoshi Kahn-Woods, constantly affirm my path as an entrepreneur, insisting that I am successful, even in those moments when a path seems to end.

Those of you who are "dog people" understand my need to be grateful to my golden retrievers, Lily and Maggie, whose unconditional love and ongoing companionship fill my life with positive energy, peace and joy. In their usually quiet, undemanding ways, they exemplify the words "relationship" and "giving."

Mom, you have always been my foundation. You taught me about the power and importance of community, giving and inclusion. You and Dad, even back in the '50s and '60s when most girls were told that their options were limited, insisted that I could accomplish anything that I put my mind to—talk about lessons in persistence, optimism and confidence. I am a strong woman because you are a strong woman. I say a mere "thank you" knowing that you know what I mean.

My Significant Other, John Lamie, if nothing else, has taught me how to not take myself too seriously, which, given my ultra-serious personality, has been a stretch. But your irreverence, deeply kind and loving nature, plus wisdom as a business and sales coach provides me with a continual sounding board, kick in the butt, *laughter,* and the love I need to be independent, dedicated and connected. Thank you ...

Finally, my children, Edwina and Ron, and their spouses, Matt and Nicole, who challenged me to finish this book by each getting married in the middle of the writing process. The four of you honor me by pursuing your unique paths, establishing yourselves as strong independent adults and exuding love for me, our family and each other. I cherish you and feel blessed beyond description.

The exorbitant length of these acknowledgments reminds me that I couldn't be who I am without others. My heart-filled thanks to all my relationships past, present and future.

Introduction

Who here wants to succeed? Silly question, of course. We all have our own very personal definitions of success and most of us are united in the quandary of how to achieve it. Welcome to a conversation that I hope will make you excited and optimistic about business development. Let's start with the punchline: It is DOable, and it is a myth that we need blood, sweat and tears to acquire the gold ring. Whether you are a new or mid-career partner, a beginning or senior associate, the concepts that I am going to share with you will help you advance toward your personal and professional goals—whatever they may be. The centerpiece of *all* that is to come is *relationships*. You have experiences developing relationships, right? The same approaches you have used to make friends, find life partners and engage job interviewers can be put to use to advance your legal career. The keys are to turn your social skills back on (one lawyer once told me that they were bred out of you in law school; I don't believe him!); develop a strategic mindset comprised of *what* you want to accomplish and *who* can help you get there; and devise a daily implementation plan that fits your very unique strengths, comfort zone, values, goals and way of living.

Not convinced it's doable? You're not alone. The legal profession, and law firms in particular, has an ambivalent attitude toward business/relationship development,[1] which, no doubt, has impacted you. For example, what is emphasized, almost exclusively, in law school? The knowledge and skills needed to provide stellar service to clients. What activities are rewarded most heavily in law firms? Your billable hours and the quality of your substantive legal work. Yet, lawyers who *exclusively* follow this course of practicing law limit their chances of advancing their careers. What is emphasized from the beginning of your career is only one piece of your success equation. Success in most law firms requires high-caliber *professional* skills AND the acquisition of business.

---

1 Throughout this book *business development* and *relationship development* are used interchangeably. Less experienced lawyers can use the system described to grow relationships that can help them immediately obtain important substantive experiences and assignments. Later in their careers these relationships may lead to business or connections to business.

Most of us who attended professional schools, be they to pursue a career in the law, medicine, psychology, film, fashion, etc., at some point hit a life-changing moment when we realize that in order to earn a living doing what we most want to do, we need to understand business and relationships in some way, shape or form. For many of us who have run from any kind of activity that involves selling, this is a frightening and horrific discovery. I will never forget a dramatic moment of coaching a fifth-year partner in a large law firm when the need to generate business became real for her. Spontaneously she started yelling, "No, no, no, no, this isn't why I went to law school! I don't want to be a salesman, I want to practice law! They have betrayed me!" She characterized her outburst as a "business development temper tantrum" and further shared that she didn't want to be a "sleazy used car salesman" who pushes products on friends in order to make money. Can you relate?

I promise you, this book is not about turning you into one of "those." I am going to give you a very simple, three-step framework for rainmaking success and then give you lots of ideas to color "inside the lines" with YOUR personality, YOUR comfort zone, YOUR values, YOUR goals, etc. so that making rain will become a natural extension of what you do on a daily basis—nothing forced, phony or sleazy. I will introduce you to ways of developing business, creating new relationships and expanding relationships with people you have known for a while, that many people find are fun and enriching. Impossible? Intriguing? Let's get started.

Part I

Business Development—The Big Picture

We all learn in different ways. I like having a foundation and general context of what I am about to study before doing the deep dive; so that's where I am going to begin. This chapter starts with you. What is your motivation for being a business developer? Your purpose is your driver.

Next are some essentials: the building blocks I will use throughout the book, the economic climate that surrounds your rainmaking efforts and an introduction to the model that frames the discussion to follow.

In relationship terms, let this chapter be our "introduction phase," a time for you to gather first impressions, warm up to my ideas and see if you want to move ahead. Very important: this book presents *one* way of developing business and relationships ... there are many ways by many smart people. As you read Part I assess how the concepts resonate with you. If you begin to imagine yourself using the ideas, that's a great start for continuing our relationship. If we don't quite connect during the first few pages, I hope you will continue on. What I will be presenting to you is not a "cookie-cutter" framework; all ideas require your personalization, style and decisions about implementation. In other words: Just add YOUR Way.[2]

---

2   With attribution to John Mitchell, with whom I co-created YOUR Way programs through our work together at KM Advisors.

Chapter 1

Why Do Business Development?

How would you answer this question? The most candid response I regularly receive is "Because the firm requires it." That doesn't sound very motivating to me. A case in point is Sally, a dynamic woman who had been a partner in a midsize firm for seven years. She called me for strategic business development coaching with the following introduction: "The senior partners in my firm think very highly of me. They would like me to assume a major leadership role within the next three years, but to do this I must have a substantial book of business. They think I have the smarts and skills to lead the firm, but they can't make me a leader without business, so, they are paying for business development coaching to give me the credentials I need." Sally was excited about working with me and we got started immediately. However, progress was not easy.

All of my coaching sessions conclude with me asking, "So, what homework are you assigning yourself?" Each meeting Sally gave herself homework that she characterized as relevant and accomplishable within the time pressures of her busy schedule. Her second session began with Sally vehemently apologizing for not having done her homework. She stated that a new complicated client matter interfered with her being able to attend to the self-assigned tasks. She reassigned herself the same activities for the upcoming week. The third meeting again began with Sally apologizing for not doing the work. I calmly told her that no apologies were needed, that our work together was about discovering ways to consistently integrate business development concerns into her complex life. We created a plan based on taking small daily actions that she determined would utilize minor increments of time. "Yes," she said, "there is no reason that I can't do this." And, as you are probably anticipating, the following week nothing was done. Now, Sally was feeling terrible, embarrassed and thinking of stopping coaching. I decided to change the conversation. It sounded something like this:

Me: Sally, tell me the truth, do you really want to develop business?

Sally: Absolutely, yes, of course.

Me: Why?

Sally: Well, I love what I do, so more business is a good thing. And it is important to the firm, and I need it to become a leader.

Me: So one of your main reasons for doing this is that it is required by the firm?

Sally: Absolutely. Being a valuable member of the firm is important to me and I want to be a leader.

Me: Are there any other reasons that you want to bring in business?

Sally: Well, of course there would be an increase in my comp, so that's always nice. But money really isn't my main driver. I love being a lawyer and having interesting cases. Helping as many people as I can is what I care about the most.

Me: That's super. I can really hear your dedication to what you do. If it's okay with you, let's focus on the comp for a moment. If you could bring in so many cases that your comp went "through the roof," how would your life be different?

Sally: Wow, I don't know, I have never thought about it.

Me: I don't believe that. What really big dreams do you have that would be impacted by a huge comp?

Sally: First, I would be a major leader in the firm and that is the most important. Now the "silly" things—or maybe they aren't so silly, just personal: I am going to think really, unrealistically huge, okay? I would open two savings accounts with $500,000 in each; one for each of my children, so they could pursue whatever education they want and not go into debt. Next, I would buy one of those huge, beautiful, glamorous houses on the beach and have a driver that would bring us all there whenever we wanted. And—now this is really frivolous, but you said that was what you wanted to hear—I would give myself an allowance of $5,000 per month to go to a spa, buy something extravagant or just have luxurious fun and relaxation.

The conversation continued about the value of what Sally considered to be her dreams. Until she said the following: "I never connected business development to myself personally and certainly never thought about what I want." She got so excited, she wrote down key words of each dream on small Post-It notes and put each one on the bottom rim of her computer monitor so she would see them constantly. Sally never again failed to complete her homework assignments. "When I don't feel like taking five minutes or whatever to focus on an action item, I just ask myself, 'Do you *really* want the beach house, or whatever, or not?' and I remember what I have to gain by taking the action I don't feel like doing at the moment. I now know that business development is a highly personal pursuit, not because the firm is 'making me do it.'"

Sally's lesson about business development being a "highly personal pursuit" is an important message to incorporate into your own rainmaking considerations. The drive that helps all of us achieve any goal, whether it is to run a marathon, lose weight or learn a new language, is fueled by elements that are important to us. What images, desires and goals kept you motivated to complete all that you had to do to get into law school, succeed in law school, pass the bar and obtain your current job? Like Sally, knowing your motivators will allow rainmaking activities to be relevant and important to you.

Start by answering this question: If you were able to triple your comp, how would your life be different?

Having asked this question hundreds of times, I have discovered five major categories to consider. When presenting the list to a group, I often say before mentioning the areas, "Think of it this way: there **is** an 'I' in business development," to emphasize the importance of thinking about yourself, as a play on the oft-used statement about the importance of people working together, "There is no I in Team."

INDEPENDENCE: Where you work

IDEAL: How you practice

IMPACT: Your ability to impact others, the firm, the profession

INDULGENCES: Special things you give to yourself

INCOME: Money to contribute to lifestyle, debts, others, charity, etc.

Independence: Having a sizeable book of business optimizes your ability to make career choices. Do you want to change firms? Would you prefer to be a solo practitioner, perhaps start your own small group practice that focuses only on your practice area or industry, utilizes a particular approach to business (such as totally based on alternative fee arrangements) or is even comprised mostly of people with whom you truly enjoy working? Having a large book of business could enable you to put money aside so that you could move into a lower-paying job at Legal Aid or a not-for-profit entity or a lower paying in-house position. If you are able to put enough money away, you could even leave the practice of law entirely with minimal impact on your lifestyle and begin a different kind of business or maybe even retire early. I worked with a tenth-year partner at a large law firm who religiously put a significant percentage of her comp aside so she could follow her dream of becoming a high school teacher without sacrificing the lifestyle she had developed as a highly compensated lawyer.

Ideal: What does your ideal legal practice look like? What do you do on a daily basis? Where are you doing it? What clients are you working with? What issues occupy your time? When you are financially productive, firms are less apt to care how often you work from home (or your ski lodge). A large book of business takes the pressure off only fulfilling firm needs and ways of practicing and instead personalizes the how, what and where of your practice. You can say "no" to difficult clients who frequently want you to work on last-minute deadlines (of course you refer them to other colleagues who need the hours) and in their place have time for clients who are easier to work with and possess interesting issues. Want to do more pro bono work? When you have a significant flow of clients, the pressure to "bill more" diminishes, allowing you to make contributions of your knowledge and skills as dictated by your values. In summary, freedom expands as you demonstrate your economic value to the firm.

Impact: Many clients with whom I work want to effect changes in the ways their firms operate, such as ways that, comp is determined, training occurs, experiences are assigned, people are included, etc. Since rainmaking is typically the entrance requirement to firm leadership, business development is essential in order to affect impact. One client was concerned that, at her firm, women became equity partners less often than men. She wanted her future business development success to position her to challenge and change systems she believed hurt women lawyers. She also wanted to be able to vote for deserving women who sought partnership. Describing her current status at the firm as a "worker bee who grew other people's practices," she became motivated to attain the role of "lioness" to impact her firm to change in what she thought were important directions.

Indulgences: Does talking about indulging yourself make you a bit uncomfortable? You're not alone. After I presented a talk about business development to a group at a law firm, some people shared they were uncomfortable talking about *things* that money could *buy* them if they expanded their business development accomplishments. And yet, when we speak further, frequently a playful gleam comes into their eyes when they allow themselves to "dream big" about travel, summer homes, designer clothes, hot cars, etc, that they dare not verbalize to others. Interestingly, these luxuries are easy to list when fantasizing what you might do if you won the lottery and harder to imagine attaining as a result of hard work. As someone who is not a lawyer but works closely with lawyers, I am constantly impressed by the magnitude of the time, pressures, concentration and knowledge expended by lawyers at all levels on a daily basis. This perception makes me sad when I observe how difficult it is for many of you to reward yourselves with even occasional, simple indulgences. I want to encourage you to choose at least one, even modest, indulgence to work toward bestowing on yourselves when you engage in expanded levels of business/relationship development efforts. Integrating fun into your goals adds an important ingredient to the intense outlook that typically surrounds your professional activities. Allowances aren't just for children. You work hard. Giving yourself a gift of whatever size fits your value system says that *you* recognize the rigor of your own efforts, and even if no one else knows how difficult things feel some days, you know how hard you are working and that you are proud of yourself.

Income: A final motivator to explore is money itself. People are very different in how they think about what they make. For some people the monetary number itself is a mile marker of success: it says how much they have evolved ("I made more money than last year") or that they occupy a higher position on the numerical ladder than others ("I make more money than Bill"). For others, a particular number, such as one million dollars, is a "bucket list" item, something they would just like to do for the sake of doing it. For others, money has significant, tangible value to pay off debts, create retirement funds, provide for aging parents, establish education funds, jump-start a dream business or make sizeable contributions to charities.

Business guru Jim Collins, in his books *Built to Last* and *Good to Great,* humorously (yet pointedly) discusses having huge goals, BHAGs, as essential features that distinguish great from good companies and companies that last from companies that fold. He introduced the notion of BHAGs:

A BHAG (pronounced bee-hag, short for "Big Hairy Audacious Goal") is a huge and daunting goal—like a big mountain to climb. It is clear, compelling, and people "get it" right away. A BHAG serves as a unifying focal point of effort, galvanizing people and creating team spirit as people strive toward a finish line. Like the 1960s NASA moon mission, a BHAG captures the imagination and grabs people in the gut.

Replace Jim's focus on teams with your individual efforts. Create BHAGs that capture YOUR imagination and grab YOU in the gut. Remember that the **I** in business development creates the drive that you need to thrive.

Chapter 2

Formulas for Success—Rain by Numbers

When I learn something new, it is important to me to know where I am going. If this is true for you, the following few pages will help you become oriented to points to come. If you are a learner who is distracted by previews, skip on to the next chapter.

The daunting nature of business development concerned me for the first many years of my career teaching and coaching about business development. The complexity of trying to figure out ways to put all of the strategic and execution pieces together, despite the valiant efforts of many colleagues and me, kept success elusive and frustrating for many. Because I feel so strongly that success must be attainable, I continued on a quest to figure out a way to make rainmaking doable and, in so doing, condensed several critical concepts into concise formulas. Along the way, the image of one of my favorite childhood toys came to my mind: Paint by Numbers. This was a terrific activity for a child, like me, who lacked any artistic talent, but desperately wanted to create a masterpiece. The Paint by Numbers kit contained several cards containing the outlines of pictures and a batch of numbered pencils. Every object in the picture had numbered divisions that were to be colored with a corresponding numbered, colored pencil. All I had to do to make a picture that my mother could hang in the kitchen was color within the lines (not an easy task with my personality and skill) and use the right color pencil.

I offer the following elements for you to color with the specifics of your legal practice and relationship network. In the pages that follow, I will provide a lot of information about the information below. For right now, here is an outline and the numbers.

In the current law firm economic climate and beyond, success in law firms requires the acquisition of 2 components (one is not enough):

> Strong area of legal expertise

A large network of value-based relationships

The strategy for making rain and relationships has 3 steps that must be followed in sequence. Determining:

WHAT I want to accomplish in my practice

WHO can help me get there

HOW I can form lasting, valuable relationships with my WHOs

There are 2.5 categories of WHOs:

BUYERS (or users) of legal services or other things that I want

CONNECTORS to the above

A HYBRID of both (this is the .5)

WHOs are spread among 4 "buckets":

People INSIDE your firm or organization

CLIENTS past or current on whose matters you have worked

Your PERSONAL and PROFESSIONAL network

An INDUSTRY or GEOGRAPHIC focus

There are 3 vehicles to use to sustain relationships:

E-MAIL, which can take as little as 60 seconds to provide value

The TELEPHONE, which takes a minimum 10-15 minutes in order to be interpersonally effective

IN-PERSON visits, typically the most time-consuming

Relationship development involves learning about 4 aspects of an individual:

FAMILY—whom they consider family

OCCUPATION—what their work entails

RECREATION—what they do for fun

DREAMS—aspirations they have

Note: the above spells Ford, like the car.

You have now seen the numbers: let the "painting" begin!

Chapter 3

The New Normal Business Environment

I date the "new normal" at January 1, 2000. Is that the actual date? No, but it is a round number and, at least, marks an occasion on which many of us looked ahead, ready for new ideas, new ways to live and work and new adventures. So, if you will indulge me, let's accept that date as the beginning of "new."

What made things new? More, easier and cheaper modes of transportation made it easier to be in touch with clients that previously were outside our "area," so that in a relatively short period of time we could meet with anyone, anywhere. The Internet became a vehicle for good news and complex news. Communication became fast, easy and inexpensive. In other words, previously latched gates opened—our clients are now anywhere and everywhere, the marketplace is open and huge.

The Internet and huge advances in technology across all sectors brought with them new complex issues, new products, advances in manufacturing, outsourcing, banking and finance intricacies, etc., all leading to a huge explosion of legal issues. The explosion of mergers and acquisitions brought with it business entities that were larger and more multifaceted than ever before, and legal issues, across practice areas and subpractice areas, multiplied.

And, finally, in response to all of this (which only describes the tip of the iceberg of changes), law schools graduated larger numbers of lawyers.

Being an effective businessperson, whatever your area of practice, requires that you adjust your approach to changes in the marketplace in terms of both the services and expertise needed and the available universe of buyers and potential buyers. Therefore, you, in the business of law, must maintain an awareness of a few key realities in this "new normal":

1. Legal work is highly complex and, more often than not, cannot be handled by one person alone. It is, therefore, essential to know how to effectively collaborate with your colleagues both inside your firm and inside your client's organization. For many lawyers this is a shift in approach from a period when most work was handled individually.

2. The size of businesses and the plethora of legal issues potentially facing any one client means that business development opportunities can be best accessed and acquired through collaborative efforts among lawyers and across practice groups. Developing business is most effective and efficient when lawyers work together, know each other's skill sets, trust each other's work and are aware of how to recognize issues outside of their own area of expertise.

3. The practice of law is no longer only a "practice" where individual lawyers service clients one issue at a time. It is now a highly competitive, high-stakes business where large groups of professionals "race" to obtain the most lucrative clients. Therefore, lawyers who strive to be highly valued by their firms must maintain rigorous focus on their area of expertise AND business development plan.

4. Acquiring legal work occurs over a prolonged period of time. The presence of an enormous number of excellent law firms and highly competent lawyers places increased emphasis on long-term relationships between "buyers" and attorneys. The reputation alone of the law firm and lawyer is not enough to attract business. Therefore it is essential to sustain relationships over long periods of time. "Pushing" relationships via advertising and conversationally touting one's (and the firm's) accomplishments are less effective than "pulling" relationships via cultivating connections through listening for needs, and, over time, proving yourself to be an expert who is also easy to work with and is a personally/professionally caring, nice, authentic human being.

Success in the new normal can be boiled down to having two major components:

- **A strong area of legal expertise**
- **A large network of sustained, value-based relationships**

You need both to advance toward your goals.

Chapter 4

Making Rain Isn't a Big Deal

Are you thinking, "Easy for you to say"? Believing that developing business is a HUGE deal that takes a great deal of time has kept many of you (and me) away from even trying to attract business. Throughout this book I want to help you incorporate the idea that developing business does not have to be an enormous, time-consuming enterprise. Rather, most of the time, it can be a series of small, daily actions that can be woven into small pockets of time and even into the typical flow of your personal and professional pursuits. The keys are to learn how to implement smart (time-respecting) approaches, utilize your own natural way of developing relationships and integrate a constant awareness of other people's personal and professional needs into your conversations if you aren't already. Most often, five minutes a day can foster significant business development momentum.

Building on What Works

I believe that all professionals must evaluate their work periodically. That's what I do at the beginning of every January. In 2012, the score card I gave myself was mediocre: the workshops I conducted on business development were okay conceptually, but when I transferred the information to coaching, the material didn't seem to translate into the outcomes I intended and truly wanted. The lawyer-participants needed something more and different.

Embracing the notion that business development is a behavior, something that we do, I used my background as a psychologist to research organizations that are successful at changing behavior—any behavior, not just business development.

Sure enough, there are two very well-known organizations that have achieved excellent levels of success. Let me give you a pause to guess what they are …

No, not Facebook, LinkedIn, the ABA, Apple or Netflix (common responses to my query). You're thinking way too hard if these were your answers. The two organizations that have impacted the day-to-day behavior of so many people in the United States and around the world are Weight Watchers and Alcoholics Anonymous.

Again, using my "psychologist hat" I thought deeply about these two organizations, asked myself what things they both do to help many people establish new ways of conducting their lives and wondered if the two organizations share any approaches. Many ideas came to mind; however, two stuck out most dramatically: 1) both define target behaviors in simple, basic ways: for AA it is sobriety, not drinking alcohol; for Weight Watchers it is moderation, eating a measured quantity of food; 2) both count the incidence of desirable behavior: AA counts days and years sober; Weight Watchers counts food points. Of course other elements also make both successful, yet these two impressed me as important, basic components.

With this in mind, I moved ahead to ask: How I could utilize the winning formulas to increase the amount of business development activity in which lawyers engage? First, I asked: What basic behavior drives rainmaking? My response: Engaging in relationship development. In today's legal marketplace you need to know people in order to be hired; they rarely just appear. Second, what desirable behavior must occur constantly in order to acquire business? The answer is: Frequent valuable connections with people. I admit that the word "valuable" *is* open to various definitions, much as when I was in Weight Watchers and had to choose what points would lead me to my weight loss goals (for me, eating 22 points of French fries had a different impact on my body than 22 points of fruit and vegetables), but that is where personal learning and experience becomes an important element in the process of becoming a rainmaker.

Here is the two-pronged formula that I believe is guaranteed to make rain:

1. **Possess a constantly growing list of people who will help you.**
2. **Connect with these people often and smartly.**

We will build upon these points throughout the book.

Chapter 5

Relationships, Relationships, Relationships

(Inspired by the too-early departed journalist Tim Russert, who said "Florida, Florida, Florida" was the pivotal state to win the 2004 presidential election)

Yesterday, a client told me a story about diligently courting a client for over eighteen months: "The client, a general counsel, told me that she wanted to engage me to help her company with a large matter. This was the first piece of work our firm had ever received from this company. She asked for an engagement letter and then asked for my assurance that I would receive full credit for the work. Of course I was thrilled that she was sensitive to firms having rules about who obtains credit for client acquisition. I asked her about her insistence. She explained that 'several male partners' had been pursuing her work over the years but that none of them took the time to get to know her or her company. 'All they wanted was my work,' she explained. Of course it thrilled me to know that the time I have spent getting to know her over many occasions resulted in both a professional friend *and* origination credit."

There is nothing I can say that captures the spirit and focus of this book better than this anecdote. Spending consistent time really getting to know people and letting them get to know you is, first of all, fun and enjoyable, and second (or whatever order you want), can take you down the path toward your goals, which for many of you include business.

For those of you who like mantras, the following one describes the business development "game":

The person with the <u>most</u>, <u>value-based</u> <u>relationships</u> wins.

Consider keeping that in front of you as shorthand for the longer business/relationship development strategy that we will discuss.

Part II

The Business Development Three-Step

Having not received much, if any, training in how to create a thriving business in graduate school, it is natural for most of us to adopt a haphazard, random approach to growing business. Random doesn't work: strategy is essential. As an "outsider" to the legal profession, I am struck by the irony that lawyers are brilliantly strategic and focused when pursuing their clients' needs, yet are scattered when pursing their own. That stops now. There are three steps to successfully and efficiently accumulating business. These steps must be followed sequentially and comprehensively in order to move ahead smartly.

What—does a successful career look like?

Who—will help you accomplish success?

How—will you create relationships with your WHOs?

Let's get started.

Chapter 6

WHAT

Your WHAT is a clearly worded, specific description of what success looks like to you, specifically with regards to the business aspect of your practice: whom do you want to work with, where are they located, what industry(s) are they in, what are the size of their businesses, etc. The clearer your vision, the more proficient you can be in designing a strategy that will take you exactly where you want to go. Your WHAT keeps you focused and less easily distracted by opportunities that seem interesting yet are not relevant to your ultimate goal. I keep my WHAT statement posted in clear view—it is a constant reminder of what I want to occur and seems to cheer me onward.

There are several tasks we need to accomplish to craft your WHAT. Let's start at the end. Take a moment and imagine your retirement party. In this scenario you have had a career that exceeds your expectations. Your career was fulfilling in every way. You enjoyed the people with whom you worked. The subject matters were fascinating. You learned a great deal about many aspects of the law and business. The firm valued all that you accomplished. And, most of all, every day was stimulating and fun. Sounds great, doesn't it? It can happen.

Take a moment and write down a description of this phenomenal career. You will get the most out of this exercise if you are specific and at least include the following aspects (try to ignore any inner voice that says. "This is SO unrealistic and impossible!"):

Clients: What exciting companies and/or industry sectors do they come from? How large are the companies?

Issues: What issues are you working with on a daily basis? What is your expertise?

Stature: Are you a local, regional, national, geographic, country-centric or worldwide expert?

Now put this information together into a few sentences. It might sound something like this:

I am THE go-to lawyer specializing in trade secrets for companies that produce computer hardware and software in the state of XXX. Large and midsize companies come to me to make sure that their intellectual property is safe from internal as well as external threats. I have a team of associates and junior partners who rigorously work with me to stay abreast of all that is going on in my practice area as well as with my clients across all of their business concerns. My relationships with my clients are so long-standing that they even consult with me on personal issues. I am truly a trusted advisor. My career has been expansive, never-a-dull-moment, fun and, yes, lucrative.

Having a vision so specific scares many lawyers with whom I work. They fear the narrow scope, saying that such limited bandwidth will eliminate work related to a variety of possibilities and therefore they will miss opportunities. This "cast a wide net" desire is common, yet not efficient and effective in terms of developing business in the long term.

WHATs can be industries (such as the fashion industry or the auto industry); they can also be geographies (such as wanting to be the lawyer that everyone in your town goes to, or specifically focusing on a country or continent). Some lawyers' WHATs are affinity-group-specific (such as Middle Eastern women entrepreneurs or up-and-coming Argentinean bankers). Your WHAT guides you to make decisions about events to go to, people to meet, issues to learn about, trends to discuss, etc. It typically encompasses a direction that distinguishes you from most, a practice area in which you are (or could be) an expert and a direction that you would enjoy.

After you have crafted your WHAT based on your passions and interests, it is time to add some reality to the picture so that you know you are headed toward an overall goal that is possible and fits your practice circumstances. One new partner found the above exercise really illuminating. "I never thought about what I really wanted," he said. "I was so focused on making partner, my own wants never entered my mind! What I would really LOVE to do is be a lawyer for major league baseball." This revelation initiated a lot of discussion between us: did he want to work with baseball teams while being a lawyer in a law firm or did he want to transition his career to a position inside an individual baseball team organization? Another individual shared a WHAT that was currently outside of her firm's strategic business development objectives. We discussed ways that her desires could potentially fit and expand the firm's direction and the importance of sharing her goals with firm leadership. In this instance, the firm was delighted by her creativity, but this is not always the case. Should you discover a mismatch between your definition of success and your firm's, you have a choice: consider other WHATs that will provide elements of satisfaction, or consider a plan to move to a venue where you can pursue a direction that is important to you. Take your time, think through options, speak with people you trust and move forward slowly.

Before moving on, share your WHAT with people you trust inside and outside the firm. Ask them what they see might be the challenges to accomplishing your WHAT. What resources, knowledge and information do they think you might need to have in order to be successful? In a moment we will discuss the various WHOs that can help you achieve your WHAT, but before moving on, it is important to make sure that you can articulate a WHAT that is accomplishable within the scope of your work setting and the business world in general. (For example, if your WHAT is to make lots of money, and you're exclusively helping small farmers comply with regulatory statutes, you may need to do some rethinking.)

A few final words on your WHAT. First, don't move forward with other parts of your strategy, the WHOs and HOWs, until this is done. Second, it is possible to change your WHAT. This happened to me. I had a very clear vision of what I wanted my coaching practice to look like when I began this part of my career. I pursued it rigorously and followed all of the steps systematically. What happened? Despite receiving a lot of input from a variety of sources, I incorrectly assessed the desirability of my services. So, back to the drawing board—new WHATs, WHOs and HOWs. Was this a waste of time and effort (three years!)? No, I learned a great deal, made many connections and became older and wiser. Finally, it is important to commit your WHAT to writing. Your WHAT is your guide for your strategic thinking. Place it in a prominent spot; use it to propel ahead.

Chapter 7

WHO

I t is interesting to me how natural it is for most of us, across all professions, to think about HOWs before WHOs. HOWs are actions such as writing an article, presenting at a conference, going to a networking event, asking a general counsel to lunch, etc. It often feels good to do HOWs, as we can "check the box" and say that we did something. *I cannot encourage you strongly enough not to think about HOWs yet, no matter how tempting.* I promise we will get there. Without clearly knowing your WHAT and WHOs, your actions will largely be random, likely inefficient and frustrating.

Your WHOs are people, companies and organizations that can help you achieve your WHAT. Knowing your WHOs allows you to pursue business from many aspects of your life cognizant of whom you want to meet and to whom you would like to be connected. Clarity about your WHOs helps you assess if you are in the "right room" because your WHOs are there. Knowing your WHOs allows you to clearly inform others about whom you would like to meet so they can help you navigate the "connections highway" to become acquainted with people who can be instrumental to your success.

Before we plunge more deeply into this important, second aspect of your strategy, I want to remind you of the mantra I introduced earlier:

The person with the most value-based relationships wins.

In this section of the business development conversation I want to focus intensely on the word "most." We covered the word "relationship" earlier and you are no doubt clear that relationships comprise the heart of your business development strategy. Let's talk now about "most." As I write this section I am smiling, as it was inspired by my father, who died way before his time at age sixty-six. I was blessed to have him as my father and mentor for many reasons; among them is that even prior to the women's movement, he insisted that there was "nothing I couldn't accomplish." With respect to achieving goals, he called on one of his favorite pastimes, baseball, and said, "Winning is all about how many times you get up to bat." Such is also the case with developing business in this competitive marketplace—it is a numbers game: your ability to succeed is directly proportional to the number of people with whom you create strong relationships. As we move into this strategic area, I want to encourage you to take this advice and think as expansively as you can so that you can get up to bat many, many times.

Your WHOs List is an expansive compilation of individuals and organizations that can help you succeed. The list, which will begin to create in a moment, must be long and thorough. It will expand throughout your career. Can it be too long? Basically no, as the length is inspirational and provides options and opportunities. As we move into the HOWs, you will find that the plethora of names gives you choices about actions to take and people/entities on whom to focus. For example, when I travel, I look at my WHOs List to see who lives in the city I am going to. Periodically, I look at my WHOs List to refresh my priorities. Your WHOs List will help you plan whom to talk to at a conference or firm meeting, whom to gather together for lunch or a roundtable discussion and whom to send an important article to. Having a WHOs List enables to you make action decisions quickly, as you possess a centralized repository of your relationships and individuals with whom you aspire to have connection. There is no pressure to connect with everyone on your WHOs List at any particular point in time; it is merely an organizational tool that facilitates creative and effective action.

The "Rain by Numbers" pages earlier in the book contain two important formulas that we will use now.

There are 2.5 categories of WHOs:

> BUYERS (or users) of legal services or other things that I want
>
> CONNECTORS to the above
>
> HYBRID of both (this is the .5)

WHOs are spread among 4 "buckets":

> INSIDE your firm or organization
>
> CLIENTS past or current on whose matters you have worked
>
> PERSONAL and PROFESSIONAL network
>
> INDUSTRY or GEOGRAPHIC focus

As we develop your WHOs, please note that your WHOs can be aspirational people or companies with whom you would like to connect and/or people you already know with whom you would like to expand the relationship.

Developing a WHOs List

Different systems work for different people. Appendix A contains a copy of the WHOs List we use at Threshold Advisors. Note that it is a simple Excel spreadsheet. Having worked in a medical setting, I imagine the names listed vertically on the left-hand side of the page are "patients". Each "patient" then has a few columns where key information is recorded, and then, moving across the page horizontally, there is space for recording outcomes of specific actions, as if, as a hospital doctor, I recorded information on my daily visits with each patient. You can obtain an electronic copy of the WHOs List at www.DauntingToDOable.com on the Tools tab.

I use a paper version of my WHOs List. I have about fifty pages, legal size, in a binder. For me, having this list at my fingertips allows me to easily grab it, plus, it is never out of my sight as it might be if it were stored on my computer. Those very tech-savvy among you may find the form more helpful on your computer or tablet.

If you have your own system, or an idea that you think will work better for you, by all means try it. Making rain will happen most successfully if it is strategized and conducted in a way that fits your personal style and personality. There is only one wrong way: that is an approach that doesn't facilitate **your** process.

Bucket 1: Relationships inside the Firm

Relationships inside the firm are the cornerstone of your success in general. These are the individuals who vote for your advancement, provide billable work, connect you to all sorts of valuable individuals and give you the support, mentoring and guidance you need for complex and everyday issues. Think of your WHOs inside the firm expansively, across all roles, levels of experiences, practice areas and offices. The importance of these relationships is huge and, in my opinion, very underexplored and underutilized. Consider this small list of ways that relationships inside the firm can help you advance your career:

Experiences to increase substantive experience

"Cross-selling" opportunities

Substantive and business development research help

Models/teachers for practice and business development

Introductions inside and outside of the firm

Inclusion on panels

Co-author articles

"Buddy" coaching/action accountability

Positive buzz about you, your work, your accomplishments

Support

Answers to questions

Responsibility sharing

Fun (we mustn't ever forget this)

There are many examples of progress that lawyers have made when increasing their awareness of the value of their peers. Here are a few:

1. When coaching a partner on the East Coast, I learned that she was interested in working in an industry in which she had enormous enthusiasm and few direct connections. Ironically, a few weeks later I began coaching another partner, from the same law firm on the West Coast, who had just joined the firm, having been in-house for ten years in the industry of interest to the person on the East Coast. Neither partner knew that the other existed, much less their mutual interest. I introduced them to each other. They are now pursuing business together.

2. I worked with an individual who had been a litigation partner in his firm for eight years. He was discouraged at his lack of progress in developing his own clients. Throughout our work together I asked him what businesses he thought were most vulnerable to litigation in the next five years. He identified an area that had never been pursued by the firm. When bringing up this potential focus in a partners' meeting, he received the following comment from a transactional colleague: "It's funny you should bring that up. I was considering exploring that area, but didn't want to do it on my own." Together they are creating an industry-focused WHOs List.

3. A senior associate was feeling pessimistic about business development because she, as yet, lacked the expertise to attract clients. Thinking that she might not

be the only one in her firm to feel this way, she, on her own, announced a teleconference for all senior associates in the firm to explore how they could support each other to pursue business. The response was enthusiastic! A large number of the group decided to begin an initiative to establish relationships with their in-house peers and create ways that in-house and firm lawyers could help each other advance.

Start making a list of people inside the firm with whom you would like to begin or deepen a relationship. Use the following prompts to help you think comprehensively:

Individuals in your practice area, at any level, in all offices.

Individuals from practice areas that might "feed" your practice area. For example, if you are a tax lawyer, you might want to get to know more individuals in corporate areas.

Partners in any practice area who have clients in an industry that you are considering making a primary focus.

Peers, from anywhere in the firm, who would be a good fit for you as business development "buddies."

Established rainmakers to learn from.

"Power players" in the firm.

Professionals who can provide valuable business development information, research and guidance, likely people who lead business development efforts. Also consider the librarian.

Partners about whom you have thought, "I would really like to work with her/him," but don't know how to make this connection happen.

Conceivably, you could put everyone in the firm on your WHOs List. Don't panic; after you form your list, you will determine a priority system. I have one client who decided that it was important to her to get to know more individuals who work on transactional issues in the financial sector. Given the size of her firm, she decided as a first step, she would like to know women partners in this area. She spent the summer reading a few bios per day to determine whose experience might best match her direction. She also reached out to a few partners she already knew and asked them who among her list were easiest to work with. These were "high-priority WHOs." When she moved into the HOWs (action), she asked for introductions.

Among the best reasons for working in a large law firm is the huge potential for collaboration. The comp structures in many law firms and other political realities sometimes make relationship building difficult. Positioning yourself as someone who is truly interested in others, has integrity and will give value rather than take it will inspire trust and attract people to you.

Bucket 2: Past and Current Clients

Relationships with individuals (and companies) for whom you have provided (or are providing) excellent services are often referred to as "low-hanging fruit." These individuals make the easiest "picking" (relating) for a few reasons:

1. They already know you and have confidence in your services

2. You know various individuals in the client company, or know the individual client her/himself

3. You understand their business to some degree

These various points give you ideas about potential "next steps," such as needs that the individual(s) or company may have going forward in addition to ways to valuably sustain the relationship(s) with key individuals.

No matter what your role in a particular piece of legal work, or your level of expertise, relationships with client individuals are important to maintain. If your conversations were mostly with less experienced lawyers, becoming interested in their career advancement can allow you to become an important colleague throughout the years. If you had tangential but pleasant connections with business leaders, maintaining these connections could lead to sources of professional support or even introductions later on. And, certainly, if you have been a leader on a matter and conversed with another leader, the two of you have many ways you can assist each other on an ongoing basis and even become friends.

I am frequently asked about ways to professionally maintain connections when a matter has concluded if the piece of work was not "yours." The answer to this varies with firm cultures and mores. That being said, trust within a law firm is best created and maintained when individuals leading efforts and "in charge of a relationship" are kept apprised of all communication that happens within the sphere of a given client. If you are ever in doubt about whether initiating contact with a former client or individual related to a client is appropriate, it is always best to ask the individual coordinating the client relationship.

Before developing this part of your WHOs List, it is important to consider some of the ways that past and current clients may contribute to your rainmaking efforts and even to your career in general:

Provide introductions for other work inside their company

Act as a connector to relationships inside their industry

Supply knowledge about challenges and opportunities in the business

Supply knowledge about challenges, opportunities and trends within the industry

Become a client, should an individual client move to a different organization

Be a conduit for career opportunities inside the client organization

Act as a connector within trade organizations

Become a powerful source of praise inside your firm about your work

Develop a rewarding professional friendship

Start this bucket only with names, unless you have easy access to up-to-date contact information. The following can help you get started:

1. Ask your assistant, your billing department and any other department in the firm that is responsible for recording your work to provide a list of client matters on which you have worked.

2. Confine your initial list to the past five years as a way of prioritizing.

3. If you have practiced for a long time and changed firms, creating this list might be challenging. One individual I coached told me that she had to go into her attic to find her "old boxes." This effort was impressive but didn't have to happen at the beginning of creating her WHOs List. Start with the most recent and accessible records.

The next step is to discover where each of these individuals is now. The Internet, Google and LinkedIn will be your best friends to accomplish this task. If you can delegate, even better! Remember, business development is a "small deal"; attend to this task in small time increments. This activity also does not require that you use your very technical legal mind, so consider searching for current information while watching television, when supervising children's homework (this is Mommy/Daddy's homework) or when you are tired but still productive.

Finally, remember that you will never be "finished" with your WHOs List. It is a document that will evolve throughout your career and be usable no matter its length. Consider this Phase 1 of WHOs development and confine yourself to a limited number of WHOs from this bucket, such as twenty-five, about whom you have complete information. Add to it as time allows.

Bucket 3: Personal and Professional Network

The undervaluing of people's personal networks has often made me pause dramatically during presentations. For example, there was the senior associate that asked if it counted (I love that phrase, "Does it count?") that his childhood best friend's mother was currently being groomed to be the CEO of a Fortune 50 company. A new partner asked me if she should have a business talk with her uncle, the inventor of a major household product, and my other favorite question was about a sister-in-law who was a top leader in a major financial firm. According to this partner, he had never told her what he did for a living (needless to say, that was remedied and business ensued).

The concentric circles depicted on the following page[3] represent different tiers of people in our personal and professional network. The circles closest to the center are people with whom we are usually closest, starting with people in our family and extending to people one degree of separation away: friends of friends.

Our personal/professional network is a resource that must be leveraged for many reasons: first, in most cases because of the personal connection, they want us to succeed; second, they can be the source of many important introductions, especially colleagues outside the firm who might need local counsel, know of speaking opportunities or fabulous job prospects and, of course, are important sources of support.

---

3   For a colored version of this chart, see the Resources/Tools section at www.DauntingToDoable. com/Tools

Personal/Professional Network Circles

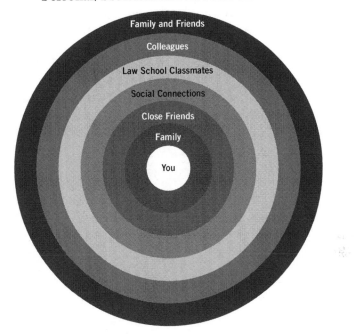

There are several potential challenges in accessing the business development value of your personal and professional network:

1. Most of them (and the people you meet at social gatherings) don't understand what you do. "Lawyer" means trials, personal injury, DUI, divorce, wills and issues that are apt to touch them in their personal lives. However, most of you practice in focused areas that impact businesses. Legal profession vocabulary such as IP, M & A, SEC, regulatory, transactional, and practice group names (to name a few phrases) are meaningless to many in your personal world. To help you and connect to you, people in your networks must understand what you do.

2. Many of them hear that you are so busy and overwhelmed that you don't want work (if you can imagine that).

3. Most don't understand the comp system that impacts your ability to succeed. You may feel an urgent need to bring in business, but they think you are on a fixed salary and don't understand that bringing in business is critical to your success profile.

4. Most lawyers I have worked with feel "slimy" and "opportunistic" even seeing family and their social networks as sources of or connections to business, so they take this relationship bucket off their WHOs List entirely.

In the HOWs section of the book we will address all of these challenges. For now, trust me that each is surmountable. Right now, let's populate the WHOs List in this bucket. Start with individuals who occupy the first circle, your family, then add names for each of the next circles. Make notes about whom each might know, what each does for a living and during the day (even if they go to school) and don't eliminate individuals whose focus is the family and home. Everyone knows people.

During my conversations with lawyers, many have downplayed the potential influence of their families. For example, one woman lawyer told me the following story: "I am the first person in my very large family to graduate from college, much less law school. This makes me different from most of my colleagues who have been brought up with friends from powerful families, families that own businesses and could be great clients. This puts me at a huge disadvantage."

I responded by asking her about the occupations of her various family members. She responded that her parents and eight aunts and uncles all lived locally and owned restaurants and hair salons. "Hmmmm," I responded dramatically. "Who do *they* connect with on a daily basis?" Her face brightened. She got the point: her family members were in direct contact with potential clients and strong sources of other introductions! Our conversation moved on to adding their names to her WHOs List and, later on, how to help her family become connectors.

Our children are also "one degree of separation" from potential clients and connectors. One of my clients laughs at the business conversations she has had over the years on the soccer sidelines. Others initiate important relationships waiting in the day care line or volunteering for the school auction. Each one of you will have different feelings and opinions about having business development discussions with family and friends. Remember that there is not one *right* way to being a rainmaker, just YOUR way. Use this book to help you consider the infinite ways to approach developing business and starting conversations beyond what you have done so far. As we will discuss often, success requires that you experiment with behaviors outside your comfort zone. These efforts may move you forward or fall flat. Failure to engage those in your personal and professional network decreases the number of times "you get up to bat." Together, through the conversation in this book, let's find ways you can say "yes" to new discussions and approaches. For now, as you list WHOs, consider the *potential* of those who are currently around you and whom you have met in the past, such as law school friends, influential people in your college alumni association, colleagues with whom you have been on a panel, etc. Hold your skepticism and fear of HOWs at bay—just list. See how many times you could get "up to bat" if you found YOUR Way? On days that I feel down about business development, this particular bucket lifts my spirits as it reminds me that possibilities exist. I just need to give myself a little push to make contact.

Industry or Geographic Niche

Let's start this discussion with the all-important question: how do you pronounce N-I-C-H-E?

Broad research on several dictionary websites indicates that "nich" AND "neesh" are both acceptable pronunciations. With that critical issue behind us, let's move forward.

For the purpose of our business development discussion I define niche as follows: *A clearly defined group of individuals, usually in a specific industry sector or sometimes a geographic space, on whom you focus relationship development efforts.* An industry niche allows you to repeatedly interact with a specific group of people and companies and focus intensely on their business needs, areas for growth and trends. Since you don't have the time and energy to thoroughly learn about every business, a well-defined industry niche allows you to gain deep exposure to people and knowledge so that you can develop the sustained relationships needed to be known and trusted. When utilizing geographic and affinity group niches, it is important to clarify specific criteria of inclusion, such as individuals/businesses in a given city, region, country or continent or African American women, male CFOs, Baby Boomers, etc. Your direction will be even clearer if you can define an industry or interest area subset within the niche such as entrepreneurs, bankers, medical device inventors, etc. The more similarities you can find among people and industries in your geographic or affinity group niche, the easier it is identify issues and people that the niche occupants have in common. This allows you to leverage time, relationships and knowledge and create or find venues in which to interact with people within the niche.

Often lawyers call their practice areas "their niche." I suggest a change in nomenclature: use the word "niche" to refer to your business development focus area, the area in which you spend non-billable, business/relationship development efforts. Call your area of expertise your "practice area." This distinction allows you to potentially have two areas that can distinguish you and allow you to describe yourself along the lines of the following example: "I am a patent prosecutor who has a particular expertise in the film industry."

Having an industry niche doesn't fit everyone's practice. For example, for attorneys working in the antitrust, appellate, bankruptcy and white collar areas, an industry-focused strategy isn't effective. However, it is essential that lawyers in these areas still have a clear, directed strategy. If you are in any of these practice areas, generate your strategy based on WHOs from the other three relationship buckets. Particularly think about people from other practice areas inside the firm or in your personal/professional network who have, or are likely to have, clients who need your expertise. For example, an appellate lawyer from a large firm with whom I am working is putting together monthly conversations with senior associate litigators from her firm. As these developing attorneys get to know and trust each other, they will be well-positioned to work together and give each other work. Another attorney with a particular expertise in the ERISA area went to a conference where there would be ERISA generalists. His goal was to identify colleagues who did not have attorneys with his particular expertise in their firm so that he could provide an important service extension to their clients. Therefore, he actively researched firms and individuals that met these criteria for his WHOs List.

So, you get the importance of having a niche and are now thinking about what would be the **perfect niche** for you. This is one of my favorite discussions; so many lawyers with whom I work look for and expect **perfection**. Don't get stuck here; let's just look for a strong, viable niche—actually, several potential niches. In a moment I will introduce criteria that determine a viable niche, but let me jump ahead to let you know our direction: I want you to come up with three to five potential niches, niches that meet the criteria that I will present in a moment. Then I am going to ask you to research these niches to find one that you would like to experiment with for six to twelve months. If the experiment is successful, you are fostering valuable connections that you predict can lead to business. At this point you can give yourself the green light to move ahead for the longer term. Slow, contemplative experimentation with a niche allows you to determine if your hypothesis about the business and relationship development potential of the niche is accurate before you take a huge amount of time and energy to become an active member of the niche community.

Here are points to consider in identifying a niche that will propel your business development efforts forward:

1. **You are interested in the overall businesses and issues of the niche:** This is an area in which you are going to immerse yourself; you are going to be reading articles, having lots of conversations, being alert to issues in the media, etc. The more you enjoy the area, the more motivated you will be to spend time learning and conversing. One of the wonderful things about being a lawyer is that all businesses and individuals need legal expertise at some time in their lives; therefore, lawyers are relevant contributors to all niches. The question is, then, is the niche a good market for you? We'll come to that in a moment. As you begin to define your niche, start with an area you would enjoy: wine, cars, health care, emerging countries, finance, etc. Now let's see if it meets other important criteria.

2. **They have needs for your practice area:** While everyone needs a lawyer and you could and should acquire business that you give to lawyers in your firm outside of your own practice area, the niche in which you are going to spend the greatest amount of your business development time should be one in which you believe that your knowledge and skills are needed. If you are a health care litigator, niching the auto industry doesn't make sense even if you love cars. If you are a patent prosecutor, niching an area where there are few products doesn't make sense. Think about the challenges and preoccupations of the niche(s) you are considering. If you wrote an article about your practice expertise, would anyone in the niche be interested?

3. **The niche meets as a group/trade association, has websites, newsletters, etc.:** Meetings, websites, newsletters, etc. provide opportunities for you to become known and provide value. Gatherings offer efficient occasions to see the same people periodically and become an active part of the community. While some geographies and affinity groups possess these criteria, they are less common than within industry niches. If this is the case with your niche, you might want to think about ways to convene people in your niche, create informal newsletters, etc, so that you still have the opportunities presented by stronger industry niches. As you evaluate niches, keep in mind that the more you can connect with people in the niche, the stronger the business development potential.

4. **Possesses economies that can meet your fees:** You work at a large firm where your fees have been set high. There is limited opportunity for you to convince

firm leadership to decrease your fee as "an investment in something greater down the road." If this describes you, you must make sure that the majority of individuals and businesses in your niche can pay your fees; emerging restaurants and many new companies are not for you. Research companies with revenues that match the size of the average client in your firm. Google "Largest Companies in XXX Industry." Remember, you are entering a niche for the purposes of generating business opportunities. If they can't pay your rates, they don't fit for you.

5.   Your niche has a substantial number of companies/individuals with whom you can do business: You must be able to get up to bat often; the larger the niche, the more the opportunities. You can get a sense of numbers within a given niche through researching trade association member rosters and often just posing a direct question on a search engine.

Answers to Frequently Asked Questions and Issues

My marketing approach is based on my practice area and area of expertise in several particular subject matters. I spend time generating ideas for articles, identifying places to make presentations and accepting all opportunities to publish. What do you think about this approach?

First, let me congratulate you on taking the time to come up with and be committed to a plan. You are now ahead of most of your peers. However, you have skipped what I believe to be an important step—the WHOs—and have jumped right to HOWs. My concern for you is that by not thinking about your WHOs first, you will be spending a huge amount of time looking for places to present yourself, via articles or speaking, and little time focusing on developing *sustained* relationships. When you present yourself across so many different audiences, the message about your expertise will typically be heard only once by a given individual. Your potential impact is therefore diluted. In today's legal marketplace, people must know that you have the capability to meet their needs AND that you are the kind of person they want to work with. This happens only through multiple points of connection. The more you have a focused WHO, such as an industry, the more chances you have to spread the message about yourself and your expertise to the same group of people, in different ways, over time. This increases your rainmaking power. Remember, your ability to succeed depends on the SIZE of your WHOs List and the NUMBER OF TIMES you are able to be in touch with a given individual. Articles and speeches are great HOWs, but you need to clarify your WHOs.

I am a health care regulatory lawyer and have worked with all kinds of organizations from all over the health care sector. Your concept about niche is interesting but, in my case, the health industry is huge. What do I do?

Great observation! Most industries need to be "sub-niched," including yours, energy, food, retail, etc. Pick one part of health care: large hospitals; physicians in a particular area of medicine such as cardiology, urology, etc.; or service delivery units such as assisted care facilities, urgent care facilities, specific laboratories, etc. There is no *perfect* subsection for you as long as the sub-niche:

- Has needs that fit your specialty.
- Meets as a group/trade association; has websites, newsletters, etc.
- Possesses economies that can meet your fees.
- Has a substantial number of companies/individuals with whom you can do business. Three hundred is a good minimum.

You don't have to be a medical expert and know all their vocabulary and understand their medical procedures. However, you must know enough to communicate how what you do can help them mitigate challenges, create opportunities and enable them to do what they do responsibility and legally. The more you understand about their business and the trends in the industry, the more valuable you will be.

In my firm it is all about origination credit, bringing in new business with companies with whom the firm has never worked. We are not even given credit for expanding work with existing clients. All of the companies with whom I can work already have ongoing relationships with firm senior partners. This keeps me from developing any kind of "book." What should I do?

This is a tough one and certainly creates a compelling reason for firms like yours to change their comp structure: you feel discouraged and therefore not motivated to even think about business development. Please don't turn away from this focus. It is essential to satisfy some of your own *"I"s* (remember earlier in the book about the five *"I"s* of business development). Independence, for example, can occur though the relationships and business that you have. Here are some points to consider:

1. Remember that you can bring in work that is outside of your practice area. If you identify a legal need through social conversation, this could be a source of origination credit for you. We'll talk more about this later in the book, but

for now, I will plant this seed: when you are at social events, think like a legal generalist, someone with knowledge across the entire legal profession. This will help you hear a potential legal need, even outside your area.

2. Research says that client loyalty is diminishing, including with clients that were once considered to be "institutional clients." While all of the "key" relationships may seem "taken" right now, remember that people leave organizations and retire. Having relationships with up-and-coming leaders may position you for work later in your career.

3. Consider developing relationships/business among companies "one degree of separation" from the one that is being served by senior partners. These businesses include vendors, suppliers and consultants to the original one. Moving into this space allows you to leverage your knowledge and expertise and maintain connection to the traditional area while at the same time developing your own, new direction.

4. Think about relationships on your WHOs List with whom you can develop industry knowledge, connections and individual and business knowledge. While this may not foster origination credit in your current firm, I have found that informing leaders inside the firm, particularly during comp time, about the depth and breadth of your relationships with clients documents the fact that you have value to the firm.

5. If you have discovered other ways to deal with and think about this challenge, please let me know. I will share all responses!

Forming Your WHOs List

As you begin to develop your WHOs List, it essential to remember that **this list will be with you throughout your career**—it is a never completed, constantly expanding document. Therefore, do not succumb to common mistakes that will keep you stuck, such as **only** working on your list, and not beginning any HOWs, until you can't think of any other people on the planet that should be added. If you do that, you'll suddenly find yourself 100 years old and no longer practicing law.

I would suggest **beginning with twenty individuals or organizations in each relationship bucket** and then spend ten minutes each week adding people. Also, add people as you become aware of them, for example, if you read an article about a CEO in one of your niche businesses or you met a new, interesting partner at a partners' retreat with whom you would like to collaborate or connect further.

Decide whether you would like to work with your WHOs List in a **paper or electronic format**. There are pros and cons to each. Your choice should fit your way of working.

What information do you want to include on your WHOs List? Some people only record names of individuals and/or companies because they have contact information in Outlook or some other convenient place. Some people put information on the list such as the city in which the person works, the industry, place they met originally, etc. Others keep basic information that they want to refer to frequently, such as the names of the person's children, job title, etc. Recording dates of connection and plans for next contact on your WHOs List is important. This allows you to develop momentum and create a mechanism for sustaining relationships.

Keep extensive notations about conversations in a journal. Later in the book, in the discussion about HOWs, I will share ideas about the kinds of information that you want to keep on hand and track so that you can maintain valuable conversations that have continuity.

If you have an assistant, consider using him/her to record information and notify you about next steps. One of my colleagues brings small cards with him to meetings. He writes notes about people he meets on cards (legibly) and gives them to his assistant to transfer onto his WHOs List and other places where he records detailed information. One of my clients uses her assistant to track many of her WHOs on LinkedIn and keep her apprised of changes that they may make or comments they post. Your assistant can be an effective adjunct to your relationship efforts. Talk to him/her about what you want to accomplish and see what ideas he/she may have to help you.

Niche development requires thought, research and experimentation. Whatever industry niche occurs to you to enter, now consider it to be an *experimental niche,* one that you will work with for about six months. In about six months evaluate the niche: have you begun relationships? Are there issues in which you can be valuable? What kinds of challenges and opportunities have you uncovered through reading and conversations in which you could see yourself offering value? The following are steps to take in exploring a niche:

1. Select one to three industry groups to research based on your areas of interest, clients with whom you have done work, industries that you believe have

growing needs on the horizon. When exploring, give yourself permission to research what you think may be relatively small sub-niches. See if you are right: Are they small?

2. Evaluate the niche against the following criteria (review):

   - A "contained" industry (there are websites, trade associations, members, etc.)

   - There are a significant number of businesses that possess financials that lead you to believe that they may have adequate legal spends to afford your rates

   - They possess legal needs across multiple practice areas

   - Many businesses are located within a comfortable distance from your home base

   - The industry fits within and expands your firm's strategic business objectives

3. Talk to the firm business development professionals to learn their assessment of your niche, its fit within the firm and how they can help you research the viability of this niche.

4. Conduct research to ascertain the WHOs within the industry, issues that the industry is talking about and dealing with and events that will attract leaders in the industry.

5. Attend an event with the intent of asking questions about needs and trends, noticing the presence of your competition and discovering if you like being around this group and their general conversations.

This is the end of the WHOs section of the book. There is a lot to think about and what must feel like a huge amount to do. You will be adding WHOs to your list throughout your career, so do not feel stressed to do anything more than a few names at a time. Sometimes when I feel down about work not coming in at the speed I would like it to be, I add a few names to my list. Doing this reminds me that there are possibilities and that I do have some control in the rainmaking game.

A final question that I'm sure is plaguing you: "How do I know when I have enough WHOs to begin the HOWs?" Asking this question means you are wonderfully goal oriented. This will serve you very well throughout your career and with strategic business development thinking and action. I will answer this if you promise to remember that your WHOs List is an evolving document and should grow consistently throughout your career. If you agree to this premise, I will give you a concrete answer: a good starting point is twenty WHOs in each bucket. This will give you a platform to experiment with different ways to initiate and expand relationships (HOWs) and a critical mass with which you can begin to feel relationship momentum.

Time to get started making your list!

Checklist for Creating Your WHOs

As you approach this To-Do list, please keep these hints in mind: just do a little bit at a time. It is more important to do *something* for five minutes than to do nothing; just list names and information, don't be distracted by the thought "But how will I contact them in a way that feels comfortable to me?" You will be most successful by adopting the belief that everyone can be helpful to you in some way; you just need to figure out how.

The following list of To-Dos is over-the-top expansive. It is intended to stimulate your thinking and inspire you to think of WHOs that you might not have considered before. Just get started and add names as they come to you.

1. WHOs inside the Firm—List individuals who...

    i. You want to meet

    ii. Are working with your ideal clients

    iii. Can help you advance

    iv. Would be fun to collaborate with

    v. Are great "resource people"

    vi. Are colleagues/peers in different offices you would like to know

    vii. You worked with in past matters and would like to get to know better

    viii. Would be ideal mentors

    ix. Can teach you something

    x. Have power in the firm, and are people who should know of you in order for you to advance

2. WHOs—Past and Current Clients—List

    i. Individual clients with whom you were acquainted in any matter throughout your career

ii. Individual clients who were leaders of matters whether or not you worked directly with them

iii. Companies whose matters you worked on

iv. Lawyers on the "other side" of all matters

v. For all of the individuals above, where are they now? (try LinkedIn, Google)

vi. For all of the companies above, who, inside your firm, is still working with them and about what; what are these company's current challenges and opportunities?

3. Personal/Professional Network—List

i. Family—where do they spend their daytime, whose paths do they cross during the day, who are their close friends, what organizations do they belong to—ideally, how could any of these connections be helpful to you?

ii. Very close friends—where do they spend their daytime, whose paths do they cross during the day, who are their close friends, what organizations do they belong to—ideally, how could any of these connections be helpful to you?

iii. Social connections—who are members of organizations to which you belong, where do they work—in what ways might they be valuable to you; who are friends that you see maybe once or twice a year; who are friends you haven't seen in awhile; how might they be valuable to you?

iv. Childhood friends—who are individuals you haven't seen in a long time but had warm connections with; where are they; how could they be valuable to you?

v. Law school—start with people closest to you in law school, then branch out to people in your class—expand the search to alums of your law school; where are they now; in what ways might they be valuable to you?

vi. Professional connections—members of professional organizations; colleagues from past law firms; people you have met at professional gatherings you enjoyed connecting with; speakers you have heard at professional meetings.

4. Industry Niche (remember, at the beginning your niche is an experiment)

Note: This part of your WHOs List requires that you engage in research. The following steps will help you list organizations in your niche; then you want to identify individuals inside of the organization with whom to be in touch.

    i. Google using the most basic key words such as "Largest cheese companies in the United States," or "Midsize banks in St. Louis." Put those companies on your list.

    ii. Research relevant trade organizations. See what companies and individuals are listed on the trade organization websites as sponsors, members, committee members, etc. Also note speakers at trade conferences.

    iii. Determine vendors and suppliers to your core niche area. For example, if your niche is the auto industry, wheel makers, fabric makers, etc., are vendors. Follow the two previous steps for important vendor companies.

    iv. Read or even scan relevant books, journals and research, including e-publications. Authors are great WHOs for your niche, as are companies and individuals referenced.

    v. Keep adding entries to your list through frequent reading.

    vi. Use LinkedIn as well as company websites to obtain names of individuals with whom you would like to develop relationships. If you can't find the "perfect name," such as the general counsel, start with whatever name you can find and gradually navigate toward the person most likely to make decisions about utilizing your services.

Chapter 8

HOW

N ow for the section you have been waiting for: How to form the relationships that lead to rain. You have begun your WHOs List and populated it with approximately twenty individuals/companies per relationship bucket. This is a good time to remember your mantra/objective:

The person with the most sustained, value-based relationships (your WHOs List) wins.

This mantra reminds you about the importance of having meaningful conversations, discussions in which you learn something about the other person and discover ways you can help them in all sectors of their life. Providing value requires that you maintain a constant awareness of who is around you. A client told me this terrific illustrative story about the importance of awareness. She started off with "Karen, you are going to kill me!" and then went on to set the scene: "I went to my daughter's high school graduation. Like all 'pushy' parents, we arrived at the venue two hours early to get the best seats. Of course we weren't alone, everyone got there early. The anticipation and boredom over those two hours was significant, but finally the graduation happened. At the conclusion of the ceremony all of the parents stood up to see our children recess out of the hall. Then we turned to the other parents around us to offer congratulations to them and share mutual sighs of relief. I turned to the gentleman who had been sitting next to me for three hours and congratulated him on his daughter's accomplishments. We then introduced ourselves. It was upon learning who he was that I finally 'got' what you have been telling me constantly during coaching. I found out that he was the chairman of a major—I mean major—financial institution, one of my ideal WHOs. Here, I spent two hours with nothing to do and I could have been talking to him. Kill me now!" Here is your first "HOW" lesson: talk to people around you, be curious about who they are, what they do and what is important to them and be curious and committed to find something to give. You never know …

Your HOWs are all about cultivating and constantly maintaining a keen awareness of the needs of those around you, as well as people in your full relationship network, and with these needs in mind, together with an authentic desire to give, growing and sustaining the relationships.

Part III

Your HOWs Toolbox

Successful rainmakers have many HOWs available to them. They assess each situation, person and goal to select what approach they believe will move each conversation toward deeper levels of relating.

Throughout this section, just as I do during coaching, I will provide an array of ideas, about HOW to initiate and sustain valuable conversations with connections and ideal clients (your WHOs). Being the foodie that I am, I think of my approach as a buffet table of business development items. Identify ideas that fit for you and approaches that you are willing to try. Discovering ways to make rain YOUR Way will make you the most effective business developer possible. As I provide suggestions, try to give yourself permission to *experiment* with different ways of interacting with people. After the "experiment," evaluate how you felt and the impact that that approach seemed to have on the other person. Keep experimenting until you find a collection of ways that feels natural (although new and a bit awkward at first) and authentic **for you.**

Let's get started.

Chapter 9

Being an Effective "Puller"

In the beginning of the book we talked about some of the differences between successful approaches to building business in the "old" economy and those in the current legal marketplace. I said: "Pushing" relationships via advertising and assertively touting one's (and the firm's) accomplishments are less effective than "pulling" relationships via cultivating connections through listening for needs, giving to others and, over time, proving yourself to be an expert who is also easy to work with and a personally/professionally caring, nice and authentic human being. This is a foundational point to keep in mind. It is all about relationships and connecting.

Recently, I was asked to review a practice group leader's strategic plan. I noticed the following direction to team members: "Every day, it is all team members' responsibility to generate ideas for articles, panel discussions, webinars, speeches and related opportunities to present the depth and breadth of our expertise to potential clients." What is problematic about this approach? Are articles, panel discussions and speeches ineffective business development HOWs? Absolutely not—they are great catalysts for relationships, but as a solitary activity, with no eye toward leaping from presentation to connection, their value is often minimal. Here is another example: I was brought into a firm to coach a very seasoned lawyer who spoke, apparently, 100 times per year and "wrote the book" in his area of expertise. Why did such an expert need a coach? He had no book of business. Why didn't he have a book of business with such massive exposure? Because he had few trusted relationships. He would arrive at a venue (with an entourage!), stay out of sight until it was his time to speak, and then, with a dramatic flourish, leave the site immediately. He didn't even stay to greet people and sign any of his books! Clearly, not a relationship-oriented individual—no wonder no one wanted to work with him.

Just as I was finishing writing this section, an article appeared in the *Legal Intelligencer* (March 25, 2014) entitled: "GCs to Law Firms: Employ Caution When Cross-Selling."

As if wanting their voices to be heard in this book, here are some general counsels' words on their experience of pushing:

Lawrence Hayes, QVC: "I want to make sure that you are doing things [cross-selling your firm colleagues] because you are acting in the best interest of QVC, not because you are just trying to obtain additional revenue. ... If you do it a lot, it's going to show me you're just marketing as opposed to helping me."

Mark Bullock, senior vice president of government and legal affairs at Mercy Health System: "There's a time and place for cross-marketing." Bullock said that, while he would expect outside counsel to recommend a lawyer where it identifies a potential need arising from a matter it's currently working on, it's a bad idea to try to cross-sell services apropos of nothing to a client who's focused elsewhere. "Hey, you're getting called into this litigation and oh, by the way, can I introduce you to Harry who does tax work?'" is the wrong approach to take with a client, Bullock said.

Ron Basso, General Counsel, Black Box Corp.: Basso echoed that sentiment, noting it is helpful for law firms to anticipate what needs his company might have and pitch accordingly.

What sentiment flows through all of the above: If your marketing efforts are not about the needs of "the buyer," you are pushing and judged with distaste.

On the other hand, pulling people to you begins with an attitude of wanting to help others with their needs, authentic giving. While you may be a talented lawyer who knows a lot and generates great results for clients, it is important to remember that you are "swimming" in a large pool with many lawyers who also generate great results for their clients. Being skilled is not enough. Your personal presence, warmth and interest in others, along with many other features we will discuss in a bit, comprise the relationship glue that ultimately attracts people to you and drives them to want to stay connected with you over time.

Relationships develop one step at a time. Any of you who took Psychology 101 in college probably learned a model of how relationships evolve. Understanding the progressive stages of relationships allows you to be sensitive to the needs of a relationship at different points in time and match your behavior accordingly. While connections develop trust and depth at different speeds, most relationships pass through certain crossroads as each person decides, typically unconsciously, if they want to pursue more ongoing contact.

Step 1: Contact—An initial moment, think first five minutes, during which first impressions are obtained and decisions to pursue more discussion occur.

Step 2: Connection—An interchange, or series of interchanges, that determines a desire to know the other person more extensively.

Step 3: Relationship (Levels 1 and Beyond)—Infinitely expanding/deepening levels of knowing someone across one or many sectors of his/her life. As relationship development progresses, the role(s) that each individual can play in the other's life clarifies and often expands. In the context of business development, whether a person is a potential client and/or connector becomes evident, as does whether each person is "marketing" the other or authentically cares and is willing to offer value as needed.

Step 4: A highly-developed relationship—one that has value beyond professional expertise, where one or maybe both individuals call on each other for highly confidential advice and direction across many personal and professional sectors.

The number of attorneys (and certainly business developers from other professions) I have seen and spoken with that wanted to jump from contact to client is staggering. The pressure many of us feel to find a client immediately makes the temptation to skip steps understandable. We want to say "hello" and then ask for business; that is akin to meeting someone at a party and immediately proposing marriage. Long-term, valuable relationships are slow to develop as each party gathers small bits of data that answer very personal questions such as: "Do I like this person?" "Do I want to know him/her more?" "Can I trust him/her?" "Is he/she authentic?" Deep relationships typically include an element of caring: being aware of another person's needs and giving in some way, shape or form whenever possible. Giving authentically, because you truly enjoy making people's lives better, is the centerpiece of pulling and constitutes the framework for fulfilling the fundamental business development mantra we have discussed several times in the book: "The person with the most sustained, value-based relationships wins."

It's wonderful to find people who express an idea that you've had for a long time in a way that you never thought to state it. Bob Burg and John David Mann did just this in their book *The Go-Giver:* "The Law of Value: Your true worth is determined by how much more you give in value than you take in payment." With this sentiment in mind, let's explore ways you can develop awareness and disseminate worth to others with the goal of developing valuable relationships in your professional world.

Become a relentless need-seeker—rainmakers persistently listen for ways to help others. Most (truly) are not as opportunistic as some of you may think; they truly enjoy being able to assist. One attorney told me, "When I was applying to law school, if you had asked me why I wanted to be a lawyer, I would have told you I wanted to use the law to help people. Of course I was young and naïve, but I had a good spirit. Initially, joining a large law firm displaced this spirit with the constant talk about pitching for and finding business. All I heard was 'money, money, money.' Then I got it: bringing in business and helping others actually co-existed: When I was able to help people (off the clock) personally or professionally, I would, and when they needed legal services, I would provide that."

Getting to know people, the details of their lives, their challenges, opportunities and needs requires that you attend to them in the broadest sense possible. To make this process easier, some wise person came up with the brilliant notion of dividing the "getting to know someone" categories into four components that spell the word FORD: Family, Occupation, Recreation and Dreams. Use this to help you think, listen and organize your connections:

Family—whom do they consider to be "family"? How old is each family member, where do they live, what do they do during the day, are there special family holidays, activities, pets, events, occasions, challenges, etc.?

Occupation—everything related to their job/business/what they do during the day (such as a stay-at-home parent)

Recreation—leisure activities outside of work, hobbies, special interests, what they do for enjoyment, travel

Dreams—what they would LOVE to be doing if they weren't a xxxx; if they won the lottery, when they retire?

Initiating and sustaining relationships challenge you to collect and track information in all of these areas. Constantly search for ways to help people across all of these sectors, be interested and lead with curiosity. Don't keep your focus stuck on ways to give through using your legal acumen; help in all ways that you can. For example, you hear that: someone is looking for a new home in your neighborhood, introduce him/her to a real estate agent you know; someone is going to Italy for the first time, if you have been there and have favorite restaurants, share them, if you have never been, ask family, friends and colleagues for recommendations. Help people find jobs, jobs for their children, college interview connections, etc. Help through using your own resources and/or use your personal and firm networks. When you uncover a legal need, then by all means, offer your expertise (or those of your colleagues). We will discuss ways to navigate these discussions in the pages to come.

Think of FORD as divisions in a binder with a person's name. Every time you learn a new piece of information about their family, put it in the Family section. Do your best to track information so that you can send relevant birthday and congratulations notes. Remembering information about people's children is especially appreciated, as is offering assistance, connections and resources to individuals often most important to people with whom you are relating.

Please keep in mind that giving isn't a strategy that you implement to get; rather, it is an authentic gesture that comes from a true desire to make a difference. If your giving feels manipulative or opportunistic, don't do it. Conversely, if you enjoy connecting people to others and helping others succeed whether or not you get anything in return, then go to it!

Chapter 10

Effective Conversations

What is the goal of your business development conversations? If you said something akin to "get a piece of business," you and I have a lot of talking to do. Even if you said, "Promote myself and the firm," you are heading in the wrong direction. Go back to the mantra:

The person with the most sustained, value-based relationships wins.

Also go back to the discussion about how relationships are developed: **Contact, Connection, Relationship (Levels 1, 2, 3, etc.)**. I send you back to these foundational points to remind you that business (and I think fun and fulfillment, but that is me) comes from establishing relationships. Rainmakers exude several qualities that draw people to them and sustain their relationships:

> Comfort
>
> Trust
>
> Awareness of Needs
>
> Authenticity

With this in mind, effective conversations are interchanges in which you show, through your behavior, that you possess these features.

Think about the last conversation you had with a potential client or connector. Where did it fall on the following Conversational Continuums?

Talk _____ Listen

How much did you talk versus how much did you listen?

Tell _____ Ask

How much did you tell about your accomplishments, opinions, observations versus how much did you ask about the other person's life, challenges, opportunities, etc?

You _____ Them

How much did you focus on you and your firm; how much did you focus on them, their business and their life?

This may be a frightening suggestion for some of you: Ask people around you where they experience you falling on these continuums. Often our intentions don't match our actions. Feedback is helpful and essential!

Effective conversation contains behaviors that fall just to the right of center, probably at least two-thirds of the way to the right. When you listen, if you ask about the other person and focus on them, you will be able to ascertain their needs and what is important to them. If you present yourself as a truly curious and other-focused person *plus* you learn a great deal about an array of topics and gain insight about how and where to give, you might hear that they have a legal need (which, for the direct purpose of developing business, is a good thing). However, please don't turn away if you don't hear about a legal need. Remember the word "sustained" in the mantra. Restrain yourself from thinking too short-term.

Conversations that advance relationships happen within two contexts, each requiring the use of some different skills and approaches:

- Moving forward WITHIN a conversation, where you are navigating from contact to connection to setting the stage for deeper relating.

- Moving forward BETWEEN conversations, where you are sustaining a relationship from one conversation to the next.

Within Conversations

People have many different approaches to forging relationships; the trick is to find the approaches that feel natural for you. Successful rainmakers carry with them a constant curiosity about what is important to people around them. They wonder if a person with whom they are speaking could be a connector or ideal client; they see someone doing something interesting and are curious to know what is happening; and they authentically enjoy searching for ways they can offer assistance no matter who the person is.

One of my very favorite relationship gurus, Judy Robinette, author of *How to Be a Power Connector*, told me this story. It was particularly interesting to me because it happened five minutes prior to our meeting. I paraphrase:

I was walking past the Waldorf Hotel [in New York City] on my way to see you and I saw the amazing-looking woman. She must have been 6'4", in her early 20s and very exotic-looking. I stopped as I had never seen someone this beautiful and I noticed several camera people, lights and a few make-up artists. I just had to know more. [NOTE her curiosity!] So I went up to one of the make-up people and asked who this person was. I was told that she was on her way to becoming the next "It" model, but she had yet to be discovered. I asked for her card and continued walking until I got to a coffee shop. There I called a senior editor that I know at a major magazine who I know is always looking for "up and comers." The editor was thrilled by my story and said that she was going to contact the model immediately to write a story about her!

Did Judy get business from this five minute action? No. So why did she do it? She was curious and enjoys helping others. This makes her known as "THE Power Connector." There are probably few days that Judy doesn't do this multiple times—her "titanium Rolodex" proves its value.

On to other ways to make conversations effective ...

Most lawyers have been trained to have superlative question asking and investigative skills. Remember learning about *issue spotting* in law school? Remember how asking questions to learn the opposition's (or witness's) agenda, strategies, hidden points of contention, etc, was essential to developing your case or constructing a deal? Well, the same is true in developing important connections; investigative questions and actively listening to responses lead you through important relational pathways. Think issue spotting to learn:

What is important to this person across all FORD areas?

What are this person's challenges and opportunities?

What might this person need to better pursue and obtain whatever is important to him/her?

Asking smart questions and displaying a fervent sense of curiosity displays a lot about who you are and therefore very often encourages the other person to want to get to know you better. To many people, asking questions about another person displays caring, intelligence, social flexibility and an "it's not all about me" attitude—typically positive traits. It is interesting to me how many attorneys that I meet ask me for a script to help them navigate conversations. They tell me that they go to family functions and events with friends and "do fine," but, for some reason, when asked to add a "gentle" awareness of possible business opportunities or other "gives" into their mind in all settings, they become stymied and negative. "I don't want to use my friends," or "I don't want to be working all the time," they tell me. Being curious and asking what people do "during the day" is neither of these things. I, frankly, find it very respectful and caring when people ask me about my work. Asking about and having an *awareness* about issues in which you might be able to be helpful, personally or professionally, is *not* a negative, aggressive act. It *is* a way to engage people in interesting conversations.

Your tools: listen, inquire, learn, offer and stay casual **and** stay aware that there are ways you can help all around you.

The flow of asking people questions in a friendly way while listening for a need is very similar to the game of Twenty Questions, where one person thinks of a person and the other has twenty yes/no questions to discover the identity. Here is a Twenty Questions script. We will analyze it at the end.

Is the person alive?

No.

Is the person a male?

Yes.

Was he an entertainer?

No.

Was he a fictional character?

No.

Was he a historical character?

Yes.

Was he a citizen of the United States?

Yes.

Was he a president?

Yes.

Was he one of the earlier presidents in U.S. history?

Yes.

Was he in a war?

Yes.

Was he known for big ideas?

Yes.

Did he free the slaves?

No.

George Washington?

Yes.

What do you notice about the flow of questions from this game? There is an elegant "dance" where the inquisitor asks a question, receives a negative response, then moves in an alternative direction to test the viability of the response. When an affirmative response is received, she explores this path deeper, receives a negative response and then moves in a different way. When "yeses" are received, the questioner pursues until she wins the game by discovering the identity of the mystery person.

How does this fit our conversation? No matter what your level of legal expertise, developing a strong awareness of the needs of people around you in *all* situations leads to deepening conversations. This awareness begins with "buying into the game": a deliberate decision that you are going to learn about the daily activities and interests of the person with whom you are speaking until you win—discover some part of their life where you can offer value (equivalent to discovering the identity of the secret person in the Twenty Questions game). Your inquiry will go back and forth, deeper and deeper, led by your curiosity and interest and the individual's responses.

From the game of Twenty Questions where you only ask yes/no questions, let's move on to a more realistic example. Here is a sample (albeit oversimplified) conversation with someone you have just met at a Fourth of July barbecue:

Hi, I'm Karen Kahn.

I'm Nancy Quinn.

(Social banter about the event, the weather, the host, etc.)

What occupies most of your time? (Note—at this point in the conversation I don't know if she is a stay-at-home mom, working professional, etc.)

I am in sales for an electrical products company.

Oh, what kind of products do you all sell?

The boring kind. Circuit breakers, switch boards, transformers, things that light up big buildings.

Wow, how'd you get into that?

My father started the business many years ago and it was just natural that I moved into it.

Do you enjoy it? (I heard the word "boring" so I am following up on that.)

Actually, I do, it is interesting to me, but not to many other people.

What kind of people do you sell to? (I am wondering if I am a connector for her.)

Very large manufacturing companies, office buildings, anything in very, very large buildings. In fact, we are moving into doing business with nuclear power facilities.

That's a new area for you?

Yes, as that industry expands, it seems like a natural for us.

As a salesperson, where do you start when you move into a new area like that?

That's a great question. I usually rely on cold calls to plant managers.

Has that helped you get to know many people?

Unfortunately, not many.

I happen to know a lawyer who works extensively in that area with large nuclear plants. Might meeting her be a good connection for you?

You never know, but it could. Most of the time selling starts with some kind of foot in the door.

I'd be happy to make that introduction next week. Would that be helpful?

That would be great. What about you?

We'll get to ways to handle that question in a little while.

IMPORTANT NOTE: I would have had a similar conversation about any topic. If the answer to the question "What occupies most of your time?" had been "Lately, it has been training for a marathon," I would have asked deeply about that. What might I have learned? The process of training for a marathon? That "Nancy" is looking for a training buddy or has a pulled muscle, etc.? Suppose she said, "Most of the day I am in sales, but I think 24/7 about finding a new place to live," I would have asked her about where she wants to live, if she has a good real estate agent, what kind of place she is looking for, etc. If we discussed something personal (Family, Recreation or Dreams), I might have asked her about her business at another point in the conversation if we had started to develop a connection. The more you experiment with exploratory discussions, the more you will develop a "sense" about compelling conversational directions.

What was I (imagining myself to be a lawyer and in your shoes) thinking during the above sample conversation? First, I was looking for a need. Second, I wanted to learn about her and her company. I know that ALL companies have legal needs: are they merging or acquiring? Do they have environmental challenges? How are their contracts with their vendors and employees? Do they have any IP? I could have continued exploring any of those issues. Here are some open-ended questions that could have taken me down those paths. Note, avoid yes/no questions as much as you can—they typically stop a conversation. If I do ask a yes/no question, its purpose is to get a specific piece of information that can lead me to a more exploratory direction. Since I want a flow of questions that might lead to a need, I want to keep questions open, starting with general questions and moving to more specific ones, just like in the Twenty Questions game. Here are some other sample questions that could work with "Nancy":

- Do you make the electrical equipment at your facility? [Knowing that electrical equipment carries toxic waste] How do you all dispose of the waste? That must be difficult.

- How large is your company? Are there many companies that do what you do? It sounds like the company has been around for a while [she mentioned that her father had started it]—is the company growing? What direction do you see it taking throughout your career?

- What are the biggest challenges for the company these days? With so many changes in the energy field, how is that impacting you?

Now you take a turn. What questions might you ask this person in an attempt to see what challenges and/or opportunities might be on her or the business's plate? Imagine having a ten-minute conversation that is all about her and her business. What could you ask that would enable you to learn something new about a business you might never have heard about before?

Here is a tip. Think of your conversations as a funnel. At the beginning, the interchange is relatively general. You search for what direction the person is willing to go. For example, you might want to talk about her business challenges, but when you ask something like, "So what's driving you crazy at work these days?" she responds: "I really don't want to think about work today." What do you do? Change direction: think about another element of FORD (Family, Occupation, Recreation, Dreams). Try Recreation: "Do you have any trips planned this summer?" When a person responds with an affirmative, more-than-one-word answer, proceed down the funnel to gradually more specific questions, all along searching for a way you might be able to help. There will be times when the other person is not engage-able—they may not be in a good mood, they might need a moment to themselves, they might be looking to speak with someone else. If this happens, find a friendly way to move on. Hopefully, you can land on a subject. Let curiosity lead you through the funnel. Keep the focus on the other person. Avoid evaluating yourself while you are talking: does he/she like me, think I am smart, etc. Listen, ask, learn. You can tell that the other person is satisfied with the exchange when the conversation has an easy flow back and forth, the other person speaks a lot, the pace of the other person's speech quickens slightly, a sparkle comes into his/her eye, eye contact is maintained and the other person's body posture is oriented toward you.

Remember, when at all possible, lead your questions toward discovering something that the other person might need. If after five to ten minutes you aren't learning, finding a need or having fun, end the conversation with a message about the future, such as "I look forward to hearing how the vacation went," "I hope your son wins his soccer game," "If you find about more about that new product, I would enjoy learning more," etc. Ending conversations with an opening to a future connection makes your follow-up or next point of contact easy.

Try this out with someone with whom you are comfortable. In your experiment use as many questions as possible, without sounding like you are deposing the person, of course. If questioning starts feeling awkward, switch to an "exclamatory statement" such as "That sounds terrific" or "That is something I would like to get into." Avoid moving the focus to you. If the other person asks for your experience or opinion, by all means give it, but remember your "job": find the need. The more experiments you can do with people in your family or close friends, the closer you will come to finding your own style within the context of asking questions and looking for ways to give to the other person. Some people are able to ask a multitude of questions, which puts the other person at ease; others try this and it seems forced. The spirit of the drill is to discover your style while leaning toward asking, listening and focusing on "them."

Chapter 11

To Ask or Not to Ask

Now for the question I hear the most from lawyers: "How do I know when to make THE ASK?" "The ask" they are referring to is "the ask" for businesses. Every expert seems to have his/her own opinion about the big ASK: some advise lawyers to integrate it into all of their business development discussions, others counsel a more circumspect approach.

I prefer not to ask, and instead *offer*. This may seem like semantics, but here is the difference: asking is a function of my need to get business; it happens almost randomly and sometimes comes across as desperate. Take the example of a senior associate who was told by his mentor to go to a major conference and ask every in-house counsel with whom he spoke for business. This advice did not sit comfortably with him, so he called me for a second opinion. "I imagined myself going up to people I didn't know or didn't know well and saying, 'Hi, Stan, do you have any business for me?' I just can't do this," he said with tremendous exasperation. Here was my advice:

First, never ask out of the blue. I think that is obvious; it is rude. Second, if you want to make a direct "ask," do it in the context of liking the particular company or because of your relationship with the particular in-house counsel (perhaps you are law school friends or have gotten to know him/her well over the years) because you would enjoy working with him/her. Always state a reason for the ask (beyond you feeling pressure to bring in business). Examples: "I really admire the innovative direction your company is going (or the kind of work your company is doing). If you ever need a lawyer, I would enjoy getting involved with you all." Or, "It would be great fun to do some work with you. If an occasion arises, please let me know."

There is one exception to my "avoid direct asks" rule: if the person is a close friend (in the closest circle of your personal/professional network). Because of your close relationship with this person, you can be frank about the relationship between bringing in work and success in your firm. This kind of ask is stated in the context of *your* needs: "John, I am really trying to increase my profile at the firm. The best way to do this is to bring in business. If you could send business my way, I would really appreciate it." Note that you are asking for a favor and possibly even educating your friend that you *need* business to succeed. Most people, especially those who have never been exposed to the business model of law firms, don't know how important it is for firm lawyers to originate business. A very experienced woman lawyer friend of mine who has a significant book of business told me one of my favorite ask stories:

*It was my forty-fifth birthday. I asked eight very close friends, most of whom I happened to go to law school with twenty years ago, to celebrate with me. I bought us all a day at a very glamorous spa. At one particular time we were all in a hot tub drinking martinis. During a particularly relaxed moment, I turned to one of my friends who was general counsel at a major company and said, "So, Joan, why have you never given me any business?" Much to my shock, Joan replied, "I didn't know you wanted any!" "What do you mean you didn't know if I **wanted** business? You know how law firms work!" I emoted to her, I'm sure much too loudly. "Well," she said, "I figured if you wanted some of my business, you would have asked me!" I think I almost drowned. But I did learn a lesson: I made it clear to all of my lawyer friends, clients and potential clients with whom I felt comfortable that I wanted their business.*

As you consider asks, please keep in mind comments that I have frequently received from in-house counsel who complain, in distasteful tones, about law firm lawyers who seem to "troll" conferences and seminars asking "everyone" for business whether or not they know the individual. Talk about the circling shark metaphor! Full disclosure—I have heard similar complaints about coaches and consultants!

Let's move from ask to offer. The following chart depicts a dynamic relationship among two elements that are critical in understanding and assessing an individual or organization's readiness to engage your services so that you can ascertain when an offer may be received positively. Along the horizontal line is the *awareness of a need* for your services (low awareness to the left, high awareness to the right). The vertical line depicts *motivation to engage* your services (high motivation toward the top; low awareness toward the bottom). Determining the quadrant of the person with whom you are speaking guides your actions.

High Motivation to Act/High Awareness of Need: This is the "Engagement Zone," the quadrant where needs and motivation to do something about the needs come together and you can offer. How will you know this? You will have navigated the conversational funnel and discovered a legal need. It might sound like this:

You: What's occupying most of your time at work these days?

Other: We are really excited about having designed a jacket that has very discreet earphones imbedded into the collar. This allows the wearer to listen to his/her phone without putting anything into his/her ears.

You: How did you come up with that idea?

Other: (Tells you a story)

You: What kind of feedback are you getting about the idea?

Other: We have gotten fabulous responses from focus groups.

You: So what are you going to do now?

Other: We need to file for a patent.

You: Who does that for you?

Other: The person who has done it for us in the past just left the company, so we are a bit at loose ends. (You just discovered a potential need!)

You: Can you wait to file until you hire another in-house counsel?

Other: Frankly, no, as you know, the patent process takes time and we want to be able to start manufacturing as soon as possible. (You just discovered high motivation!)

You: That's something I have done often. Would you like some help?

This very abbreviated script has taken us to the bottom of the funnel. You discovered a need and a high motivation to take action.

My highly relational style leads me choose words that keep the focus on the other person's need (Would YOU like some help with this?) as opposed to MY need for business (Could I do the filing for you?). Would the outcome be the same? In this case, probably. However, if, for some reason, the person to whom I was speaking identified someone else to do the filing, my offer would still be appreciated and the relationship enhanced. If I had made an "ask," the other person would have to turn down my request for the work, and this might be awkward for him/her, which could take a toll on the relationship. Summary of Action to take in this quadrant: *Offer Assistance*.

Low Motivation to Act/High Awareness of Need, (at least take action from engaging you): In this paradigm it is important to remember that both axes are continuums; therefore, you may speak with someone who is clear that they have a need but is not ready to act (with you or anyone else) yet. Why would this be the case? Perhaps they have not had a budget approved, they are waiting to get permission to take action from a supervisor, or they need to think about the need a bit longer. You will learn this kind of information through patient, low-key questioning (remember, this is not a deposition). Sometimes you may discover that although the individual sees a need, for example, to comply with a new regulation, they are not motivated to take action at the particular time. What do you do? Some people might ask for the business anyway and try to convince the person that they must act now. I prefer not to put myself in a position to receive a "no," as I find this hampers (not stops) the development of a relationship. Instead, I continue to ask questions until I determine, to the best of my ability, their motivation to act. If they do not want to engage me for any reason, I put them on my list as a high-priority relationship, as they have a need and, over time, I want them to see me as the kind of person that can help them. I make all efforts to sustain the relationship via providing information, ideas and resources. I jot a note to myself to stay in touch with the individual personally. I check in often, stay aware of personal and recreational preferences (if their child graduates from college I send a note), invite them to events to meet people I think they would enjoy, provide virtual introductions to others I think they would enjoy meeting and do everything I can to deepen the nature of the connection.

One particular example illustrates this beautifully. A very senior lawyer had a long-standing relationship with a bank in his area. He had done a great deal of large-ticket, successful work for them. Through conversation with an unrelated colleague he discovered that his longtime client was about to be sued. Being the responsive lawyer that he is, he called his contact at the bank immediately. He was told up front that they were going to "try out" another firm just to expand their local relationships. This lawyer was very upset. He called me about what to do—should he go over his client's head and ask for the work from the bank president? Using the above model, he experimented with an approach that was new for him: he didn't ask, he related and gave. He called his client back and offered to be helpful in any way they needed, including providing a casual second opinion off the clock if necessary. Several months later the bank took him up on his offer for a second opinion, as things with the other firm weren't going well. The lawyer asked me if, at this point, he should ask that the work be transferred to him and his firm. He decided to continue to experiment with a new style and encouraged the bank to continue with their current firm. He provided guidance about how to better utilize all that had been done over the past few months. This took very little time. The bank settled the situation. They complimented the lawyer enthusiastically. They were impressed that he acted in the best interest of the bank by providing guidance as opposed to what would have been better for him, bringing the matter into his firm. Two weeks later they gave him a multimillion-dollar matter. He claimed that he learned a major lesson about his own style. Summary of Action to take in this quadrant: *Develop Relationship*

High Motivation to Act/Low Awareness of Need: Typically these individuals are involved in start-up companies. They are invested in their ideas and/or products, know that legal services are critical to their stability and success, yet likely have little knowledge about what legal services they need at different points of their company's development. During your "top of the funnel" conversation you will hear a lot of excitement and passion about the vision of their company. As you ask more questions, you will likely hear a lot about concepts and possibilities and probably little about execution or company structure. Ask a lot of questions that are tied to legal actions, such as: Have you incorporated? Working with partners is always a challenge, how are you all managing this? What are you hoping your company will look like in the next few years (do they want to be acquired, get investors, etc.)? Remember, your questions come from a point of curiosity, not sales. As you progress in the conversation, it may become clear that these individuals are motivated to talk to a lawyer (they may or may not have the funds to pay) and what they need the most at this point in time is to be educated about immediate actions that must be taken to solidify their business. Education is the nature of your relationship with people in this quadrant. Point them to resources, perhaps offer to speak with them generally, introduce them to others who are at or have progressed through similar stages of company development. How high a relationship development priority should you make individuals in this quadrant? That is up to your strategy. You might want to invest time in a few entities, especially if you are interested in what they are doing and have a hunch that their direction is filling an important place in the market. Often, relationships with such individuals and companies can best be developed in groups by offering educational seminars, providing a series of handouts and inviting them to events. A final note: Facebook once occupied this quadrant; most of us did at some point in our careers. All relationships have value. Your challenge, and the point of these quadrants, is to help you make decisions about ways to prioritize your time and develop relationships by providing value. Summary of Action to take in this quadrant: *Educate*

Low Motivation to Act/Low Awareness of Need: Warning—do not write these individuals off your radar screen. No matter who they are, they seem not to need or want your services, but they can be connectors and even, someday, clients! During casual interchanges, learn about what is important to them and think about how they could fit into your network. While you may only see these people at social occasions, think about ways to connect them to others or find a resource that will interest them. Your brand as a person is built upon how others experience you. Foster connections, be a giving person, let people know how they can help you and your world will be a rich one. This quadrant may be your least active one in terms of business development, yet can offer you significant value personally and be a storehouse of connections. Summary of Action to take in this quadrant: *Watch/Wait/Contact Occasionally*

* * * *

In the HOWs section, so far we have talked about ways to conduct strategic conversations (the Twenty Questions funnel) and a paradigm for organizing and prioritizing your relationships. I am now going to give you ideas about ways to initiate and deepen relationships across each Relationship Bucket.

Chapter 12

HOWs with Relationships inside the Firm

The more people who like you and trust you in your firm, the more successful you will be, no matter the nature of your compensation structure. With respect to business development and advancement in general, relationships within a firm seem to be a big black hole—most cultures so emphasize individual success and action that few know each other's interests, goals and clients that they could be sharing. So, the theme of this subsection is *know who works in your firm. Be the one who bridges relationships across offices, floors and practice areas.* Here are some ideas to think about for lawyers in firms of all sizes.

1. Think about your internal brand. How are you perceived? When people talk about you, how do they describe you? If you don't know the answer, ask people. Everyone in the firm is a carrier of your brand. Don't exclude knowing anyone. People who see you casually in the lunchroom talk to others, whether or not they work with you directly. Wouldn't it be great if they said, "I don't work with Karen, but every time I see her I enjoy our two-minute conversation. I bet she's great to have on a team."

2. Take a few minutes each day to read at least one bio on your firm's website. Start with the leaders in the firm. Note anything that you have in common with them: education, clients, professional interests, places they worked in the past, etc. Have they done anything notable that you would like to know more about? Could talking about it deepen your relationship (remember, people love talking about their successes!)? You can read bios while watching TV, during a teleconference where you are a passive participant, etc. Answer these questions: if time and access weren't a problem, whom would I want to meet? What would I like to discuss with them? Is there anything or anyone I know who could help this individual? What information could I easily gather that would be helpful to them? Did I read anything in today's paper that would have value to them? How could this individual help me?

3. Within your office, casually walk by as many different offices as you can over the span of one week. If your office is large enough, walk the hallways on different floors. When you go to the restroom, get coffee or go to a conference room, pass an office and say a casual "hello." You don't have to stop and have a conversation. Also, notice what is inside the person's office (this doesn't make you a stalker). What people display in their offices are things they are willing to talk about. If you want to get to know someone, talk about those items as well as what you learn from their bio, their LinkedIn page, your intranet, Google, etc. People are complimented when others ask them about their experiences. Remember, whenever possible, give, give, give.

4. Take active notice about what matters people are working on. In what ways could this intersect with your work—do you work with the same company or a company in the same industry, or a company with similar issues?

5. Who are people's key clients? How can you help them expand work with this client? Whom might you know? What areas of your expertise might be relevant to the individual's key clients? When you see a mention of these clients in the media, drop the colleague a note. They may have seen the item already, but the fact that you took notice speaks of your value as a team player.

6. What industry seems to occupy colleagues' official (if there are industry groups in your firm) or unofficial attention? How is your area of expertise relevant to this industry? Might the two of you have an important message that can be co-presented to a trade organization, a webinar, a client alert, an article, etc.? When you see mention of this industry area in the media, especially within an industry in which you are active, let your colleague know.

7. Keep FORD in mind. As appropriate and doable, collect information about all four of these areas with respect to your colleagues. Integrating comments about Family and Recreation into casual conversations expands your relationship beyond the professional.

8. Convene virtual groups of colleagues across offices for support and/or collaboration of any kind.

When I present this material in front of an audience, I am frequently stopped by an associate who says that she is uncomfortable with the above direction. She says that if she were to follow any of these suggestions, she wouldn't feel authentic and that my instructions seem like I am directing her to "use" people. I always appreciate this comment, as it invites me to discuss relationships from vantage points that may be different for some people: intentionality, strategy, and giving. What is your philosophy of giving? If giving is a means to an end for you, then, yes, you may have a tendency to be giving to manipulate. If you like making a difference in people's lives, then giving allows you to make a difference in the lives of your colleagues. Many people feel alone in law firms due, in part, to the emphasis on individual action. Developing relationships within your firm through any of the above actions can change the culture, including the work environment for you.

Your political and social capital determines your value proposition to the firm. This can translate into compensation, assignments, opportunities, sponsorship and job security. I see taking actions such as the above, which do not have to take a lot of time (and can even be done on the way to the bathroom), as essential to your career success. Do not think of them as optional: "If I have time I will ..." Go back to the goals you wrote at the beginning of this book. The path to many will be accelerated and facilitated through expanding and deepening relationships within the firm. What of the above are you willing to do today?

Chapter 13

HOWs with Past and Current Clients

I imagine that most of you reading this book understand that serving a client isn't a one-time occurrence, and that, despite your role in a particular matter, the value of a client relationship goes far beyond the matter in front of you. With that being said, and reprised from earlier in this book, let's focus on tips about HOW to deepen your relationships with clients.

1. Every time you talk to a client, ask how they are **and listen!** I was coaching a lawyer who was so focused on the matter at hand that he never asked a client, beyond the perfunctory, how he was. At my encouragement (more like pushing), one day he asked the client how he was and found out that the client's wife had terminal cancer! Adding empathy to a client relationship is just plain human. Enough said, right?

2. When time allows, ask clients about themselves. Here are some questions to consider:

   - When you aren't leading your company, what do you do?
   - How will you be celebrating the holidays (the summer, etc.)?
   - Where will you be over the holidays?
   - Did you have fun over the weekend?
   - Have you always worked in the XXX industry?
   - What do you do to take a time-out from all of this stress?

   Often, these questions lead to learning fun details about your client that can grow the relationship.

3. Stay alert to ways to give to the client beyond the current matter. What is important to them? Know the answer to this question; it is key to deepening the relationship.

4. Learn as much as you can about your client's business. This accomplishes many purposes: understanding the context of the work you are doing can positively impact your service; you may discover other areas in which you and/or your firm can provide value; you will learn about business outside of the law. The chart below is an excerpt from a terrific book about collaborating inside professional services firms: *All for One* by Andrew Sobel. I am grateful to Andrew for his permission to share this information:

Clients:
Know Their Business

Strategy and goals
What is the stated strategy, and what long-term goals have been met?

Financial performance
What is the client's performance in terms of revenue and profit growth, stock price trends, market share and competitive rankings?

The organization
Who are the key executives? What are their responsibilities?

Key operational initiatives
What initiatives are planned for the next year? (e.g., new products, cost cutting, etc.)

Major competitors
Who are the major competitors, and what is the industry structure?

Industry and market trends
What are the four or five most important trends for this client's business?

The customer base
Who are the key customers? How concentrated is their purchasing power? How do they buy from your client?

The suppliers
Who are the major suppliers? How much leverage do they have?

Partnerships and alliances
Which are the major partnerships? How well do they function?

Culture
What is the organizational culture like today? What core values does the client espouse? What does it aspire to in the future?

THRESHOLD ADVISORS

Used with permission from Andrew Sobel: All for One, p56

© 2014 Threshold Advisors, LLC—All Rights Reserved

I recommend creating a file for each client with information under all of these categories. If you are a partner, consider having an associate work on filling in the information over time about a client he/she is working on with you. Be sure to emphasize that this is not a waste of time but a way that he/she, too, can learn about the client's business.

5. Learn as much as you can about the industry in which your client is positioned. Large companies may cross several industries. If this is the case, start with the industry most relevant to your current matter first, and/or the industry in

which you choose to place the most focus. Start such conversations by letting the individual know that you are curious to learn more about the industry. Be candid about your desire to become more involved with similar clients, when appropriate, of course. If the individual mentions names of his/her colleagues within the industry, it is fine to ask if an introduction could be made.

The chart below is another excerpt from *All for One* by Andrew Sobel. This chart focuses on the elements that are important to learn about in your client's industry. The aggregation of this information will not only assist you in your immediate work, but provides data and context that will help you initiate new relationships within this industry—what I call in this book your industry niche.

Clients:
Know Their Industry

The economy and key economic trends
What are the views of leading economists and commentators?

The capital markets
What's happening in the stock and bond markets?

Technology
What major technology trends may affect your client's business?

Management practice
What basic ideas and frameworks should you understand about perennial topics like leadership, strategy and teamwork?

Demographic trends
How will these affect the workplace and consumer buying habits?

Government and politics
How does government policy influence your client's business?

The regulatory environment
What challenges are occurring?

Legal trends
What risks does your client face? (e.g., litigation, labor issues, etc.)

The media
How do the media view your client?

Non-governmental Organizations (NGOs)
Can any NGO affect your client's business, either positively or negatively?

Used with permission from Andrew Sobel: All for One, p56

THRESHOLD ADVISORS

---

6. Ask about opportunities, challenges and goals. Here are some examples:

    "What are you looking forward to during the fourth quarter of the year?"

    "What direction do you see the business going over time?"

    "What's driving you crazy at work these days?"

"What do you see as potentially the biggest obstacles to your success?"

"What comes next after this product launch?"

7. Be aware of what is important to your client individually, what will make him/her look especially good in addition to a positive outcome to a particular matter: budget containment, an award/recognition, introductions, compliments to his/her supervisor, a new career opportunity, co-authoring a paper, panel presentation opportunities, etc.

8. If you are a new associate, start keeping a readily available list of all clients you have worked with. In addition to the list, develop a mechanism to capture all information learned such as the above. Note all of the individuals with whom you speak, particularly the ones at your career level. Keep an updated record of all of these individuals to the best of your ability. It is particularly important to note their job changes. The more active you can remain with these individuals, the more useable your network will be to you throughout your career. Send biannual notes "checking in." (Holiday cards don't count unless they contain several personal sentences.) Think of where and when it is appropriate to invite these individuals to gatherings.

9. No matter how long you have been practicing, lead your client relationships with a strong desire to learn about who they are, their business direction and their vision of success. If you are a newer lawyer and feel uncomfortable about your stature, the questions you ask say a lot about you. You don't have to have extensive legal knowledge to be seen as an impressive, up-and-coming professional. No questions are "dumb" questions. Ask about the client's experience, how he/she came to this point in his/her career, etc. Curiosity is a strong attribute. If you are in doubt, try this: "I am really curious and would love to know more about your company. Could I ask you some rather basic questions?" Most people see your interest as a compliment.

Chapter 14

HOWs within Your Personal and Professional Network

The preponderance of lawyers, at all levels, with whom I work and to whom I speak, seem to start thinking about business relationships with people in their personal and professional network and become handicapped by a debilitating fear: that talking about business means imposing on friends and therefore should be avoided. Women seem to be stricken by this more than men, but many men also share this concern. I frankly find this stance a bit strange as, to me, when people don't ask me about my career, it signals that they don't *really* want to know me—after all, a huge amount of my identity and day is about my professional pursuits. As was mentioned earlier, the antidote for this phobia is being honest with yourself about why you are conducting business conversations with friends and then, if the motivation is positive, acting accordingly and even talking about it. Ask your friends about their business and career to expand the relationship AND to explore if there are ways you can help each other.

Here is one of my rules to live by: "When in doubt, be transparent." When I am talking to a friend who I think may perceive my conversation about what she does professionally as an effort to take advantage of her or may take it negatively, I ask, "Susan, I would like to hear more about what you do at IBM. Is that okay to talk about?" Susan may respond, "Sure, what do you want to know?" or "Frankly, I spend so much time at work, when I am at home I would rather talk about anything but," or "I would be delighted to talk about what I do, but I have to draw the line on anything that would involve hiring you to do work at IBM." With all of those scenarios stated, I will confess that I have never had a friend who wasn't pleased to compare notes about our work. AND, when I add, "I have a strong belief that the best way for all of us to get ahead in what we do is to help each other. I would love to figure out whom I might know or what I can do to help you," people dive on it. In other words, people rarely turn down the offer of assistance and, I think, we all have a secret wish that someone would *offer* to help us. We are afraid of asking for help lest we look vulnerable and unsuccessful.

Now, why you SHOULD consider having business discussions with people in your personal and professional network?

1. The people with whom you have personal connections likely want you to succeed, especially people in your family and your BFFs.

2. Business conversations expand close relationships. Tired of asking your brother how his kids are doing on the soccer field? Treat him like a potential client: learn about his business, his challenges and opportunities, how can you help him, whom you might know that could help him. When you engage in these conversations, family ties become stronger and the traditional "objectives" of a family unit (surviving, love, etc.) are expanded to helping all members advance to new levels of success.

3. You can leverage the cliché "It's a small world" to advance business. We'll talk about how to do this in a moment, but first the concept: How many times are you at a cocktail party or even having a quiet dinner with a friend when a seemingly random comment about a person, college, town, even summer camp comes up and the reference becomes a point of connection? ("Oh, you work with large food companies? My sister is the EVP of X"; "Oh, do you know Selma Smith? She was my college roommate.") If you talk to personal and professional contacts about business, your "net" (as in network) can become huge. Wouldn't that be a good thing?

If these points make sense to you, read on. If you still want to draw a firm boundary between your personal and professional relationships, go on to the next section.

On the previous page I talked about ways to begin a business discussion with a friend. To repeat, if you are hesitant, ask permission to talk about business. If you are ready to jump in, here are two thoughts about beginning conversations:

1. If you are meeting someone for the first time, ask WHERE they work. I recommend steering away from "WHAT do you do" as the first question. Hearing about their place of employment opens the funnel larger. The "WHAT do you do" certainly follows.

2. If you have a hunch that the person is not employed or works inside the home, you might ask, "What keeps you busy most of the day?" Please keep this note in mind: stay-at-home parents are fabulous connectors. You never know whom someone knows and whom they interact with throughout their day. Maintain a rigorously curious mind and willingness to help with everyone you meet.

Either of these openings leads you to the conversation funnel. What are you looking for: learning new things, finding a need you can fulfill, having fun meeting someone new? Those are great benefits, of course. Here is the AND: AND, within the process of friendly conversations you might discover a piece of information, a reference to an individual, an opportunity, etc, that can help you. "OH, I get it," some wonderfully skeptical participants have said to me, "all of this giving and friendly stuff is just a cover to GET." The perspective that underscores your actions is absolutely up to you. I embrace the idea that the world is a better place when we all actively discover ways to help each other. I contribute to this notion by finding ways to help in every conversation that I can. I know that when I give; I receive what I need from somewhere else. This is not a woo-woo, Oprah-esque idea; it is just the worldview that guides my life and allows me to have the kind of authentic conversations that I do. You must find your foundational beliefs in order to act and come across as authentic.

Building my business and succeeding is also a concept that I hold dear, which I am not embarrassed to admit. This has taken me some time to "out." When I was in my twenties, my supervisor told me that he could tell that I was "ambitious." I spent the next hour apologizing and feeling terribly embarrassed. Now, older and somewhat wiser, at least more experienced, I embrace my ambitions and have decided that ambition plus the commitment to give to others and the world is a great way to live and work. Now, onward to more details about bridging personal and professional conversations.

An important challenge to address is how to talk about what YOU do. The way you introduce yourself will open or close the mind of the individual with whom you are speaking. **Don't introduce yourself as "a lawyer."** Here's a little demonstration to discover why:

What comes to most people's minds when you say you're a lawyer?

Perry Mason, the TV show *Law and Order*, any type of criminal law.

Is this how you want people to think of you?

"Ah," you say smartly, because you are, after all, a smart lawyer, "I don't just say I am a lawyer; I say I am a trust and estates (or real estate or intellectual property or complex commercial litigator, etc.) lawyer.

With all due respect, none of these descriptors makes sense to most nonlawyers. Most of us think that a lawyer is a lawyer is a lawyer. I now know better! And, while I am talking about confusing job titles, please don't call yourself a complex commercial litigator. That phrase truly is confusing, as it is such a broad characterization; it means relatively nothing.

"So what DO I say when someone asks me what I do?" you ask. I am going to answer that question with a question, a "trick" many of you great litigators have taught me to win an argument: ideally, when you meet someone for the first time, what would you like to happen?

The most honest response I get from an audience, which is always said in a very flip manner, says, "a piece of business" (laughter in agreement ensues). The second "good participant", says, "I don't really care about business when I am at a social occasion, I just want to get to know people and have fun" (empathic nodding occurs).

Here is my take on the generic, professional label introduction: responding to the question, "What do you do?" with a response that neither pinpoints your expertise nor clearly describes what occupies your time during the day doesn't help you develop a relationship or have an interesting conversation. However, painting a brief word picture, or better, telling a brief story, does.

Here's the formula I use: "You know how..." (and then I describe a situation that is easily understandable and describes the kind of matters I tend to work on); "Well, what I do is..."(I describe the work I do in these circumstances). Here is an example:

You know how one of the large shoe companies developed and sold a shoe that had a heel that was shaped into a very steep angle (or wedge)? Advertisements said that if you wore this shoe every day the muscles in your backside would tighten and look sexy? Well, it didn't work. Buyers got angry and wanted their money back plus damages. When I say this, my voice pitch typically raises at the end to form a questioning tone. If it doesn't, I ask a quick, "Do you remember something like that?" I am hoping that I chose a story that is easy to say "yes" to—meaning yes, I have heard this story, or yes, I get where you are going.

Well, what I do is help big companies who are sued by angry customers when something doesn't work as it is supposed to.

This story might have some technical flaws, but hopefully conveys the spirit of a class action lawyer and provides the listener with a pretty good sense of what a particular lawyer does. Why would I want the listener to understand these details? I want to be thought of if a similar situation arises. In addition, it is a much more interesting way to describe what this lawyer does than the generic "I'm a lawyer."

As the conversation goes forward, you can certainly name your firm, say that it does all kinds of law, etc., if you want. This conversational technique allows you to create a clear connection based upon comprehensible professional information. From here, all kinds of ways to get to know each other and help each other can ensue.

A second method to introduce yourself builds upon identifying people you may know in common ("Oh, you live in New York City, do you know my cousin Fred?") I call this the "inner Rolodex technique." For those of you who grew up in the computer age, you may not know that a Rolodex is a rotating filing device many of us used before the Internet to store contact information. In my imagination, everyone's brain is made up of a Rolodex that contains information about everyone we know or have met. In order to be connectors for each other so that valuable introductions can be made, we need to "trigger" each other's Rolodex. "Inner Rolodexes" are triggered when we are presented with something familiar, such as the name of our college, the town we grew up in or members of our family live in, etc. The more specific the reference, the more fine-tuned (and potentially relevant) will be the connection. When searching for business connections, providing a business reference might lead you to obtaining valuable connections. Therefore, when asked what you do, lead with a category of WHOs, the more specific the better. Usually, naming an industry area is the best. Name an industry you are working with, have worked with often or with which you would like to do more work. Here are types of responses to "What do you do?"

> "I work with very large cosmetic companies such as Avon, Elizabeth Arden and L'Oreal."
>
> "I am expanding my work to focus more on independent record labels."
>
> "A lot of my work focuses on midsize real estate developers in Detroit."

Often people will then ask you what you do for these people. At this point, as succinctly as you can, describe what you do, such as "I am a real estate lawyer that helps large companies negotiate leases." However, do whatever you can to put the focus back on WHOs if you can: "I am really enjoying meeting and getting to know large developers. What kind of connections would help you?"

Many people I coach respond to this suggestion with concern that by mentioning one particular industry, they are eliminating connections to all of the other industries on the planet. I understand the concern. The narrow approach is counterintuitive. You must be specific to trigger a listener's "inner Rolodex." Saying that you work for "large companies" is not likely to get you connections. You can mention a few industries that you work with, but I don't think this is as strong an approach as mentioning one. You can try it out and see how it works for you.

Chapter 15

HOWs within Your Industry or Geographic Niche

Industry niches give you the competitive edge in a marketplace where relationships plus knowledge is king. An industry expertise brings all of your WHOs together in one place in your mind. Knowledge, of all kinds, provides the currency that positions you as the attentive, valuable, caring person to go to when a need arises.

The host of MSNBC news program *Hardball*, Chris Matthews, has a request of his panelist guests that guides my relationship development with people in my industry niche: "Tell me something I don't know." Recognizing that my industry WHOs are very busy and that their focus is usually on their own business, I collect and share information about marketplace trends and practice trends about which they may not be aware. If I send them something with which they are familiar, sending the information lets them know that I am thinking of them.

Staying abreast of industry comings and goings is a time-consuming affair. There are companies that are knowledge aggregators that will compile and digest information and deliver the information to you daily. Knowing how busy you are, be as specific as you can about what you want to know from these providers or else you will be flooded with information that you never use and don't have time to read. You might want to focus on a set number of ideal clients within an industry and entities that are not already clients of the firm. Also, consider tracking key trends within an industry such as new products, mergers, etc. The comings and goings of leaders in an industry keep you abreast of corporate changes and potential transitions in business approaches and guide you to connect to new players and thought leaders.

Here is the challenge: gathering knowledge, especially since technology provides a constant stream of information to you, must be a constant and broad-based activity. How does one person accomplish this? He/she doesn't. Collaboration and team assignments are smart and efficient.

Build a team comprised of members at all levels of experience. When I suggest this to partners, they often react negatively, saying that associates, at any level, don't have time for business development. I respond, "In order to be career smart, they must." The danger of starting business development when you are a partner, or even senior associate, was mentioned early on in this book. The wise associate knows that being on a business development team with a partner provides insight on how to make rain, hands-on experience in relationship development and an opportunity to start accumulating knowledge about an industry on which he/she may focus in the future. Offer a place on your team; detect by the response whether the individual is a rising star.

Before disseminating assignments to the team, it is important to explain your goals and direction. For example, explain that as a team you want to know all the companies, trends and happenings in a particular industry of a given size and possibly also location (i.e., midsize semiconductor companies on the East Coast). Provide the group with a lengthy list of companies that is important to the team: current firm clients as well as potential new clients and a list of contacts. The more information you provide, the more effective team players can be at compiling and staying abreast of information.

After presenting a comprehensive briefing about the industry niche, engage in a discussion about where to acquire ongoing information about events within the industry. Provide a list of resources. Engaging the group in a discussion about other places they could find information will elevate the level of engagement among team members and, given younger professionals' proclivity to be aware of the newest technological tools, may teach you about new, effective ways to gather intel. (See Chapter 18 on Social Media.) The goal for an initial meeting of this sort is to develop a collaborative strategy that will initiate the gathering of the broadest amount of information that can be used for developing relationships. Some information may be relevant to only one individual/company; other pieces may be disseminated to larger groups.

The collaborative model must involve give and take throughout all activities or else members' contributions will dwindle. Everyone must feel that being on the team has value for them. The most effective teams have short, frequent meetings where everyone reports on their discoveries; all members, particularly those most involved in relationship development, share how they have used the information gathered by the team; and, at monthly, longer meetings, the team discusses ideas about ways to initiate and expand relationships within the industry.

The following is a basic list of resources from which to find knowledge. Information aggregators are not included on the list.

Individual company websites, especially sections that contain news

Google Alerts

Trade association websites and newsletters

The *Wall Street Journal*

The *New York Times*

Local, national, international newspapers

Bloomberg Business Week

Fast Company

Inc. magazine

The Economist magazine

News and magazine format television shows

Chapter 16

Working a Net (or Networking), the Intimidating Frontier

The number of venues in which relationships are developed and expanded is infinite, yet few (perhaps none) are as intimidating for most lawyers as large gatherings of individuals: *The Networking Event.* Why do we go to these occasions when the thought of attending is simply distasteful for some and brings back horrible memories of junior high school dances for others? The easy answer for many of you reading this book is that you are "forced" to go by senior members of the firm or business development departments and/or are lured there with *promises* (by experts, mentors, etc.) of riches never really well-defined. So, we go, wishing we could use the time to bill clients, go to a yoga class or spend time with loved ones. I respond to the preceding sentiments with the following statement: **Don't go to networking events. Don't go whether they are inside the firm, sponsored by the ABA, your favorite charity event, your niche trade organization or hosted by your best friend. There is no return on investment to networking events. Just Don't Go.**

Of course you are waiting for the catch. Here it is: don't go to networking events *unless* you are willing to put in the work to make your attendance worth the time spent. There are many places to engage people. You don't have to spend time with a large group in order to be a rainmaker. However, truth be known, smart attendance at large group events can be an efficient way to grow and initiate relationships. This section is devoted to providing you with an effective strategy for going to large group events. My goal is to give you a way of thinking about and executing at these occasions that will fit for you whether you are an introvert or extrovert.

<u>Think about it this way</u>: You are going fishing and want to bring home the tastiest fish you can find. What is your strategy? First decision—you want to gather as many potentially tasty fish as you can to see which is the best. Do you use a line or a net? While a line could get you quite a good dinner, you will only be bringing up one fish at a time, and they will be winners or losers. A net will yield you the largest number of fish in the

shortest time with the greatest likelihood that one will be tasty. This thinking is the reason you go to a large event. You can cast a wide net and be privy to a large "catch." Appointments with individual people provide intensive attention to one individual, which has tremendous benefit, especially when you are developing a relationship. But, at the outset, when you want to meet new people and have brief "touches" with a lot of fish, a net-event is an efficient use of time.

Second decision: you now have 200 fish in your net—what do you do to find the tastiest? This is when you must work your net, and it is work. Just staring at a collection of fish isn't going to tell you much about each fish. You need a process and criteria to help you *discern* which fish might be the best candidates to take home. Let's push this game out one more minute and list criteria that would help you effectively choose the tastiest fish relatively quickly:

1. Type (Are some more tasty than others? Do you like the taste of some more than others?)

2. Size (Are larger ones more tasty than smaller ones?)

3. Gender (Which taste better, male or female?)

4. Age (Do old fish taste better than young fish?)

5. Appearance (Spots, stripes, lots of scales, no scales, sharp fins?)

6. Habitat (Salt water or fresh water?)

The point of this perhaps silly exercise is to illustrate an effective way to think about attending what at first may seem like a generic, pointless gathering: Think about WORK when you consider going to a large event; what do you want to achieve (a tasty fish?); whom do you want to meet; how will you recognize a valuable contact; and how do you engage each person in a way that gets you what you want? There are four steps in this game plan:

1. Preparation

2. Execution

3. Debrief

4. Follow-Up

Preparation: I am often asked by my coaching clients if they should go to a particular event. The answer is straightforward: go where your WHOs are. Large events provide an informal occasion to begin to know someone, continue the relationship building process and learn about professional and personal needs.

How do you know if your WHOs are going to be there? The easiest way is to obtain an attendance list from the host or someone close to the event. If this is not possible, you need to make an intelligent guess. You can do this by knowing who has gone to this event in the past. If the event is hosted by a trade association involved with your niche, there is a strong likelihood that WHOs (remember, WHOs are ideal clients AND connectors) will be there. Often, making contact with speakers at an event is valuable, so if there will be one or several speakers, find out who they are. If none of these avenues is available to you, and event planners refuse to give you any information the day of the event (even a few names of attendees would be helpful!), then go early and look at the name tag table or ask individuals at the name tag table if you can look at the attendee list. If this isn't possible, then take a step back and ask yourself the reasons you are considering going. If your answer is "I *should* go," but you can't articulate the purpose, then don't go. Having a clear purpose guides your activities. That being said, you can still go without clear goals, as you never know whom you may meet and events may contain connectors.

It is important that you be very clear about your goals. One of the reasons many attorneys feel overwhelmed by large events is that their goals aren't clear. Ambiguous goals promote wandering around the room *hoping* that something exciting will happen—clearly not a captivating proposition. Instead, either be clear about the exact people you want to meet or, if that is not possible, specify what you want to talk about and the characteristics of the people you want to talk to, such as: "I want to talk to five in-house attorneys that deal with privacy issues about how they are managing security problems with respect to cloud computing." This gives the event a purpose, and frames your discussions, and quantifying your goal (in the above example, five in-house lawyers) tells you when you are finished and can leave the event.

Once you know your goals and WHO will likely attend, obtain research about the WHOs so that you can generate meaningful conversations. Review information mentioned earlier about business and industry topics to discuss. Possessing personal information about an individual's career can also provide excellent content for discussion. Be aware of relevant current events and, when you are in a city with which you are not familiar, it is helpful to obtain general information about what residents might be talking about, such as their sports teams, community events, local politics, etc. You don't need to study extensively, just be informed so conversation can flow.

Finally, review techniques we have discussed about conversations, especially ways to ask questions, find needs and introduce yourself and what you do.

In summary, preparing for an event provides the direction and substance that raises the likelihood that attendance will be valuable.

Execution: Compelling conversations that initiate and/or deepen relationships with your WHOs is what working the net is all about. Yet, group events, by nature of having a lot of people who want to converse, pose some difficult challenges. Here are the ten most frequent questions that I am asked about executing at large gatherings:

1. *Since I will be speaking with a lot of people, how do I remember everything about the people I talk to?* It is perfectly okay to write a note in front of the person to whom you are speaking. In fact, if you say something such as "I want to write this down so I remember to send you the article" (or ask you on Tuesday how the meeting went, etc.), it can be construed as a compliment. You are telling the person that what they are saying is SO important that you don't want to forget it. Write the note on the back of THEIR business card, in the notes section of your smartphone, or on a blank business card (a great accessory for large events). However, if taking notes in front of a person isn't comfortable for you, take several "time-outs" from the event to capture important information.

2. *If my goal is something like five conversations and the event is only an hour long, how do I fit five satisfactory conversations into the time frame?* Working the net involves relatively short encounters that are designed to pave the way for more extensive conversations in the relatively near future. Ideally, each discussion will last about ten minutes so that you, and the other party, can move on to speak with other people. As you approach the time allowance established to accomplish your goals, tell the person to whom you are speaking that you would like to continue the discussion in a quieter or less chaotic setting and ask if you can contact them in the next few days to set up a time to speak further. Here are a few ways to express this: "I am really enjoying our conversation and would like to continue it in a place less distracting. May I call you next week to set a time?" or "I have many other questions I would like to ask you. Can we talk again soon?" The key, and we will talk about this further in the Debrief and Follow-Up sections, is to establish the expectation that a next meeting will occur.

3. *What do I do if I can't seem to politely end a conversation and move on to talk to someone else?* I call this the last raft on the Titanic phenomenon—the person is gripping on to you like you are the last life raft available. Understand that this individual is probably more uncomfortable in the setting than you are, so be gentle. The kindest thing to do is to introduce him/her to someone else. Look for a person who also seems to be on their own (lost), introduce yourself (this isn't weird, you are behaving in the true spirit of networking), bring your "buddy" into the new conversation and then excuse yourself ("there is someone who just came in with whom I want to connect"), and go.

4. *How do you approach someone if they are talking to someone else?* Patiently, respectfully, politely. I suggest approaching at an angle that allows you to make eye contact with the person with whom you wish to speak. If the ongoing conversation stops, acknowledge that you are sorry that you interrupted and that you "just wanted to 'say hello' or 'introduce myself.'" Be sure to connect with both people and do your best to blend into the existing conversation.

5. *How do you join a small group that is talking and seems like a small, closed circle?* This is one of my pet peeves at networking events: a group that seems not to want newcomers. The first piece of my response to this question is to please be an inclusive networker. However, if the group you are with must stand close together to hear each other, be on the lookout for others that want to be included. If you want to join an established group, first try to make eye contact with one of the members and see if they will make space for you. If this doesn't work, stand on the outside for a few minutes and see if there is an opening in the conversation where you can contribute something valuable. Remember, most people want to meet people, so a gradual approach and joining typically isn't construed as pushing and not okay. Always use your intuition. Sometimes a group is constituted of people who haven't seen each other in a while and are engaging in a personal catch-up conversation. It is tough to join such a discourse. Quietly walk away and connect with these individuals at a later time. Most of all, don't take your "exclusion" personally.

6. *What are the best ways to start a conversation with someone you don't know (and who wasn't on your list)?* Identifying information is the norm in United States gatherings. It is almost perfunctory, as few of us remember people's names unless we repeat the names several times (a great practice). Therefore, briefly introduce yourself using identifying information (Karen Kahn from Thresh-

old Advisors). Next, making reference to the gathering itself establishes a point of commonality. Consider one of these (some relatively standard, a few a bit more experimental): "Is this the first time you have come to this event?" "What brings you to this event?" "I looked at the name tags coming in, there seem to be people from fascinating companies here." "I see from your name tag that you work at xxx. Is that a fun place to work?" (Or, if you have heard or read about that company, ask about it.) Comments intended to get both of you smiling and empathizing, such as "It sure is crowded here," or "Will they run out of wine by the time we get there?" work as well. The keys to a friendly beginning are to be positive, friendly and oriented to finding a point of similarity. Then move into exploring and connecting.

7. *I'm an introvert and not at all comfortable in large groups. How can I make networking not excruciating?* One of my very closest colleagues and I used to go to events together. He insists that he is an introvert, but to watch him engage, well, he manages it well. The difference between him as an introvert and me, the extrovert, is the energy required by each of us to navigate the room. In most (not all) situations, I enjoy the liveliness of large gatherings—meeting new people, moving around the room, discovering how I can help people, etc. Standing still, focusing during one-on-one conversations in a busy room, zaps my ability to attend. My colleague, on the other hand, not only dreads these events (sound familiar?), he finds it very stressful and exhausting to move from one person to another. Going together is a perfect solution: he generally stands in one place (usually near the bar) and engages people around him in fascinating discussions. I, on the other hand, scurry around the room, meet great people and then tell them that they must come over to "our spot" and meet my very impressive colleague. I deliver "the new guy" to my colleague and then move on to find the next person. Together, we accomplish our combined and individual goals.

Here are some suggestions for introverts: If you can, find someone with whom to tag team. A second important point about being an introvert is that your stamina for talking to a lot of people at one event is less than most extroverts'. Therefore, set small, clear goals, such as to speak with five people about trends that they are seeing in their industry, and then give yourself permission to leave. Since your endurance is somewhat limited, keep conversations short and your goals realistic. Third, prepare a few things to talk about ahead of time so you can initiate conversations easily. Finally, the more you practice and find a style with which you are comfortable, the easier working a net will be.

8. *I am a young associate. How do I conduct a conversation with someone much older and experienced than me and sound like someone with whom he/she would like to do business?* People do business with someone with whom they are confident and comfortable. At the associate level of your career, it is not likely that someone will want to hire you; however, they might want to hire your firm. Impress people with your curiosity and poise. Don't worry about bringing in a client as much as learning from the person with whom you are speaking. Ask about his/her business, industry and experience. If you hear a professional need, talk about how you know that your firm has expertise in the area and that you would be happy to make an introduction. As an associate speaking to a experienced individual, your goals are to ask informed questions (having done your preparation about people and companies that might be in attendance), listen carefully for personal and professional needs, practice exuding mature, personable presence and experiment with various ways of working the net.

9. *I hate sports. Do I have to talk about it?* Rainmaking requires that you relate in authentic ways. You don't have to do anything that feels wrong, noxious and extraordinarily uncomfortable. (Stepping a few paces outside your comfort zone fosters growth and is typically recommended.) So, my first piece of wisdom to you is that you have choices. My second message is that the more tools you have in your tool box, the easier it is to navigate the diversity of relationships. These tools include subjects that you can talk and ask questions about, even at a surface level. It is up to you to decide what topics you are willing to explore. Sports, movies and local happenings, in addition to industry trends and professional concepts, tend to be relatively safe topics around which most people bond. The more topics you can talk about, the easier it is to find a point of commonality. I recommend that you *scan* the local papers and a national publication such as *USA Today,* and/or listen to news on the television, to stay generally abreast of current headlines. Do you have to talk about sports? No. Do I recommend that you know who won yesterday in whatever town you are working that day? Yes.

10. *Do I have to go to large group events?* No. Attendance at networking events is *only one* way to develop and sustain relationships with your WHOs. It is an efficient mechanism, as large group events provide the opportunity to interact face-to-

face with many of your WHOs at the same location in a brief period of time. However, there is a huge menu of ways to get to know people, including but not limited to providing CLEs, seminars, designing small events such as round-tables, lunch/dinner/coffee/drinks, etc. Among the extremely important activities facing you throughout your career is designing and fine-tuning a business development direction that uniquely fits you. No, you don't have to go to large group events. Yes, you must discover and leverage YOUR Way of initiating and sustaining valuable relationships.

There truly is an art AND science to optimizing your effectiveness at networking events. The more permission you give yourself to try different tools and techniques and to stretch outside of your comfort zone, the more you will grow and find YOUR Way. Here are some last points to consider about the execution stage:

- Fight the inclination to talk only with people you know, especially lawyers you work with on a daily basis. Large group events are an excellent platform to converse with people who don't typically cross your path. Even speaking with only one person who is new to you or is someone you see infrequently successfully expands and deepens your relationship world.

- Be a connector; introduce people to others. This activity makes you the most valuable and appreciated person in the room. Remember, everyone at these events aspires to meet and speak with others. Being the catalyst, just as you might if you were hosting a barbecue at your home, gives you a concrete activity on which to focus your efforts, plus it allows you to meet a lot of people and help others.

- The best place to position yourself (with or without a drink) is near the entrance of the room. This allows you to read the name tags of people as they come in so that you can determine if they are one of your WHOs. Additionally, being a friendly, welcoming presence at the entrance of what is an intimidating occasion for many people projects a positive impression and often attracts people to you throughout the event.

- Maintain an awareness of your energy level throughout the event. When you become tired, leave; your abilities to carry on compelling conversations, maintain connection and appear engaged diminish as fatigue sets in. While not ideal, you can connect with people you missed via e-mail and phone. The return on your time investment is optimized when you communicate clearly and appear fresh and rested. Take a few moments to check in with yourself during networking to make sure that you are pleased with the way you are coming across.

Remember, a major purpose of networking is to pave the way for next conversations. (Your mantra: The person with the most sustained, value-based relationships wins.) Your efforts to continue conversations will be eased if you identify points for follow-up during your discussions. For example, someone may mention that their son or daughter is competing in a soccer tournament that evening. Either record or do your best to remember this fact so that you can inquire about it in a follow-up note. As I will discuss in the next sections, connecting next communications directly to discussions that previously occurred provides continuity, deepens the relationship and lets the other person know that you were truly listening.

Debrief: Debriefing sets the stage for a strong return on your (and the firm's) investment of time and resources. Immediately capturing all that happened at the event, including information about people you met, industry trends, business tidbits, potential legal needs, ways you were successful in drawing people out in discussion, substantive material, potential future, opportunities and ideas, moves your efforts forward. This reflection, further, enables the creation of a follow-up strategy.

Time pressures make it tempting to want to skip the debriefing step. Don't. Without it you risk forgetting important details about conversations and may even forget the event entirely. I will repeat this a few times in the next few pages: if you are not going to follow up, don't go to the event. As we have been talking about all through this book, sustaining relationships over time so that you have developed trusting relationships with people when they have a need and/or connection is the most powerful driver for success. Networking provides a launch point for the next conversation; therefore follow-up is *essential*. Given the enormous pressures on your time, I recommend this technique to help you debrief and follow up efficiently: when you place the networking event in your calendar, *also* reserve a time to debrief and follow up. You can allocate one twenty-minute segment to debrief, preferably within twenty-four hours of the event to maximize your recollections. If you take public transportation to and from the gathering, debriefing on the go is an ideal time.

Remember to add new names to your WHOs List and make notations about *when, how and about what* you would like to have another conversation, such as a phone call, visit, time at another gathering, etc.

Bottom line: debriefing events provides the mechanism that assures that all information gathered at events is saved and can be used later. Debriefing captures your relationship gold coins; don't skip this step.

Follow-up: Every time you follow up after networking little rainmaking angels dance, they know you are on the jet way to success.

Following up continues conversations begun at an event. Connecting follow-up communication to the previous conversation keeps the relationship-building process fresh. Refer to notes that you took during the event and your debriefing record to refresh your recollection about the content discussions, especially needs. Many lawyers with whom I work send "it was good to meet you" notes after an event. This is okay, but unless a "bridge" relating the follow-up to the event conversation is made in the note, this is a relatively ineffective, although polite, effort. If you find yourself stymied about how to follow up, possibly because the conversation during the event was very brief or occurred while in a large group, meaningful follow-up is still possible and important. Think about what you know about the individual or take a few moments to research the individual. What would you have liked to talk about? What might you have forgotten, or not had time to ask, mention, etc.? Think FORD. What did you learn about the person that could be a stepping stone for a next point of connection? The more valuable and personal the follow-up, the stronger you are making the relationship. Here are some ideas:

- *Resources, articles, websites* related to anything you discussed, for example: "I found a website that has a lot of information about fabulous restaurants in Florence. Let me know if you decide to go to one of them. They sound amazing!"

- *Idea about a challenge* that they mentioned: "I thought about you not having enough staff. That reminded me about my great experience with virtual assistants. Have you considered that?"

- *Introduction:* "I mentioned that my partner knows a great deal about that regulatory issue. I spoke with him and he would be delighted to get together for coffee. When might be a good time for you?"

- *Inquiry*: "You mentioned your son was about to start kindergarten this week. How did his first day go?"

- *Request*: "Thank you for offering to introduce me to Samantha, your AGC. I look forward to meeting her. I would enjoy taking the two of you out for lunch sometime soon. What does your availability look like?"

- *Desire to hear more*: "I was fascinated to hear about your plans for the new real estate development north of town and would enjoy having a quieter time to learn more. Might you be free for a beer next week?"

- *Invitation*: "After talking to you I realized that a lot of families with children the age of yours will be getting together at my house over July Fourth. Would you like to come with your family?"

- *Question*: "I forgot to ask you how the new product development project is going at your company. What's new with that?"

- *Offer to assist*: "I was so sorry to hear about the downsizing at XYZ. I would be happy to help you connect with people who might have an opening in their organization or know of other possibilities. Let's get together next week."

Successful rainmakers move through Preparation, Execution, Debrief and Follow-Up steps seamlessly. Over time and through lots of experimentation they have developed their systems, learned what forms of engagement work for them and become committed to taking the time to follow their process completely. Do they ever leave an event disappointed that their expectations were not met? Sure. Sometimes people they had hoped to see didn't show up. Sometimes they are too tired or distracted to conduct effective conversations. And sometimes, there was something more important going on at home and they realized that they hadn't really wanted to go to the event in the first place so "they weren't really into it."

While attendance at large events is an efficient way to connect with your WHOs, you must be willing to navigate the challenges of finding the time to adequately prepare, effectively move around the room, speak to your target people and even hear in a noisy venue. This activity is only one piece among many of your relationship development strategy. Use it as brief conduits for next, more focused next step interactions.

Chapter 17

Sustain!

Perhaps the most challenging requirement to developing business is figuring out ways to sustain relationships. Researchers proclaim different requirements about how many points of contact are needed to move from first meeting to business; some say seven and some say more than twenty. I say that quantifying this is an exercise in futility because if there is no need for your services, you can have one million points of contact and not be engaged. I have worked diligently to develop a relationship with a leader of a large firm for over eight years. We have gotten to know each other well, she values my opinion on the challenges being faced in her firm and, frankly, I think her firm has many needs for my expertise and services. One day she casually said to me, "Karen, why aren't we working together?" You can only imagine my frustration. "I don't know, Joanne, why aren't we?" I replied, so we set a time to talk. What did I do wrong with Joanne, as I know she is using other coaches and consultants? In retrospect, I didn't maintain enough personal contact, though I did keep my name in front of her via articles, alerts, etc. Second, given the number of decision makers in her firm, I failed to spread my influence wide enough. Assessing my relationship with Joanne has been a great exercise for me and one that I encourage you to do when there is an individual and/or business who you believe has a *high need* for your services, yet you have not been able to acquire business. Here are some points to ask yourself:

Have I developed trust, comfort and overall "liking" with the individual needed to make decisions?

Have my mechanisms for sustaining the relationship fit the individual? I have sent newsletters and valuable e-mails, but did the individual need more face-to-face contact to foster the depth needed for business?

Have I been clear enough about my value proposition or have I been coming across as a generic service provider (yet another lawyer or, in my case, consultant/coach)? You must differentiate yourself and display (not just say) that what you can offer uniquely fits a special need.

Have I been proactive enough in identifying a need that perhaps they don't know they have? Often lawyers introduce or reintroduce themselves to individuals/companies after a problem has been publicized. Believe me, when you do this, you are presenting yourself with a pack of others. When you see issues on the horizon (you do this through lots of reading and conversations in your niche), you can offer to educate people about trends they may not have thought about or ask them what they think of an impending issue. This kind of thinking and action keeps you ahead of others and is a strong differentiator.

Sustaining relationships directly through conversations and indirectly through disseminating information keeps you on people's "radar screen." We are all different with respect to the number of people with whom we have the energy to sustain relationships. This is why I strongly recommend you work with a team with whom you share a WHOs List. If each person, let's say there are four of you, agrees to sustain relationships with 150 specific contacts, then the group is maintaining a high profile with 600 people!

So what should you do to sustain these relationships? Give, give, give, give, give. With time being among the most significant considerations in your life, it is important to make smart choices about how to keep relationships fresh and advancing while juggling your billable hour requirement and, of course, providing fabulous service to clients. In other words, you need to balance what must be done **today** with ways to keep you successful **tomorrow.** Three vehicles will help you create and sustain contact with people; each one has benefits and limitations:

E-Mail (a "sixty- second" task)—With practice and attention to resources, this is your most time-efficient business development tool. Keep your eyes glued to all media outlets, including social media. When you find something that will alert one or several WHOs to an important event, occurrence, trend or mention of a relevant individual, then copy, paste and send. TWO HINTS: a) Look at your WHOs list and see how many people would find this e-mail valuable; b) Remember that developing relationships is a personal endeavor, therefore, you *must* start the e-mail with a few sentences that let the individual know why you think this e-mail would be of particular interest. Do not send an e-mail with "FYI" because that does not distinguish you. Take thirty seconds to SHOW that you care by saying something about the relevancy of the contents *and* the relationship itself. Once you get into the rhythm of doing this, you can sustain five relationships a day using only five minutes. E-mail as a vehicle keeps relationships current and uses little time. However, because the potential for two-way conversation is limited, your ability to deepen your awareness of this person's needs and expand the relationship beyond the content of the e-mail is minimal.

The most common question I receive when discussing e-mail communication is an important one: What do I do when I send an e-mail asking to have a conversation and I don't hear back? This is a very difficult and frustrating issue; especially in the legal marketplace where the amount of e-mail traffic is exceedingly large and spam filters block many irrelevant as well as relevant e-mails (yours and mine!). Some e-mail systems, like Outlook, have delivery receipt components. Mine doesn't work consistently. Therefore, without some kind of e-mail response mechanism, there is no way to know whether your note was received, put on the back burner due to lack of time in which to respond or deliberately ignored. So we, the relationally motivated sender, are perplexed and challenged to follow up in a way that won't be obnoxious. You can approach this conundrum in several ways; choose what feels best to you:

1. Follow your unanswered request with a phone call. Frankly, this solution doesn't satisfy me, because I like to send e-mails in advance of phone calls to let them know why I want to talk to them. So, if I wanted to call, I would have called in the first place.

2. Call at a time when you are certain you can leave a voice mail, and tell the person that your e-mails often get caught in spam filters (true) and that you wanted to let them know that you sent an e-mail to them about (fill in the blank) in case they missed it.

3. Send a second e-mail and pray it gets through. If you do send a second e-mail, apologize "for the duplication" in case it is the second time they receive the same message.

4. Sometimes sending an e-mail with the "High Importance" indicator gets the e-mail through the system. I hesitate to do this, however, as it feels like "crying wolf."

5. If the individual has an assistant, speak to him/her explaining the situation: that you sent an e-mail, have not heard back, would like to speak with the person at his/her convenience, and can the assistant help you make a connection. Assistants are often great contact facilitators!

6. I am not comfortable with this suggestion, but, in the spirit of being complete, I share it: send a follow-up text message telling the individual that you sent an e-mail. To me, an infrequent texter, this feels intrusive, but to many of you, this may feel like comfortable, standard operating procedure.

7. Make sure your subject line is more descriptive and compelling than "Let's set a time to talk," unless you know the person well. I have found that stating the topic of the note or, if this is the first point of connection, stating the name of the connector: "Betsy Smith encouraged me to contact you," has the best chance of getting through the crowd of e-mails.

8. Finally, don't take any lack of response personally; schedule a time, maybe in one month, to reach out again.

Telephone (fifteen to thirty minutes)—Telephone communication seems to have become a lost art form and yet, given the fact that the time commitment needed for a "telephone touch" is relatively small, the quality of the time used can be high. Because telephone communication allows you to span geographic distances, discovering YOUR Way to utilize the telephone to sustain relationships is important. I have often found that telephone contact with past clients to find out how they have moved on after your work together culminates in new business. The phrase "Funny I should have you on the phone today; can I talk to you about an issue?" happens with interesting regularity. Whether or not contact results in immediate business, it does communicate caring; after all, you are taking time to "touch base." As we covered in the discussion about events, take a few moments to prepare for a conversation. Know what you want to talk about, what questions across FORD are important and relevant and what valuable elements you want to include in the discussion.

I find it helpful to frame the time parameters casually at the beginning of a conversation, such as by saying, "Thank you for taking fifteen minutes to talk to me," or, "I am so glad we have this fifteen minutes to talk." This keeps limits on "talkers" and can put the other person at ease that you will be respectful of their time. Also consider managing time toward the end of the conversation by saying, "In our last few minutes I want to make sure to ask you (or tell you, or share with you)," or, "I'm so grateful that we had this time, even though brief, to touch base." It is your responsibility to manage the time. If the person to whom you are speaking seems to be going longer than you have time to speak, use the same technique we discussed for cocktail parties: "I would really like to schedule time to continue this conversation. Unfortunately, I have another meeting about to begin. Can we schedule more time (tomorrow, next week, etc.)?"

How do you get a telephone meeting scheduled? Some people won't respond to your invitation to talk on the phone no matter what you do. Introverts, in particular, find talking on the phone awkward—can you relate? Other people—men generally more than women, but busy women, tend to respond similarly—do not feel comfortable "visiting" on the phone. Your best chance to get them on the phone is through clearly stating the agenda and value proposition to talking instead of e-mailing. The phrase "I want to pick your brain about" has become stale; don't use it. The more valuable the purpose of the call is to the other person, the higher the likelihood is that they will speak to you and enjoy the connection.

Given current trends away from professional phone chat, I rarely, if ever, call someone spontaneously. I personally find it disconcerting when someone calls me out of the blue for professional reasons. Further, I, like most people, monitor my Caller ID and typically don't answer if the caller is not a client or someone with whom I have a close relationship (or my mother). I have found that the best way to attract someone to a phone conversation is to send an e-mail in which I state either a friendly invitation or a valuable reason to converse. Sometimes I use the phrase "let's have a virtual cup of coffee" or even "virtual glass of wine" to set a relaxed, fun tone. And, when I follow such an invitation with a Starbucks or Dunkin Donuts gift card so I "buy the coffee," my invitee is particularly pleased.

Telephone conversations (for those of you technologically advanced, include Skype and FaceTime) can go a long way toward deepening a relationship, as the exchange happens in real time, emotions can be detected to some degree and there is an overall sense of humanity in the dialogue. Using the telephone effectively requires that your voice convey warmth, vitality and genuine interest. Consider obtaining feedback about your telephone demeanor so you can make it work for you.

Face-to-Face Contact (one hour or more, up to you)—I have written extensively in different parts of this book about the strategy and tactics of effective in-person connection. Given the focus of this section, sustaining relationships, let's reexamine the guidelines for optimizing this format. In-person communication is usually the most potent of the three vehicles, as it allows all of our senses to give us input about an individual's personality, emotional state or what they are not communicating verbally but may be feeling based on body language, etc. The more skilled you become at picking up cues, the more you will learn about another person and the deeper your connections can evolve. Save one-on-one meetings for the most sensitive conversations, especially discussions about a client matter and for occasions when you most want to deepen a relationship. *One-on-one* meetings are also valuable if your attempts to deepen a relationship have been unfruitful when in a group, or have not achieved the exchange of information and rapport that you believe you want/need in order to advance the relationship. Otherwise, *group conversations* provide many benefits in addition to being a more efficient use of time than individual meetings, including:

1. Introducing people to others with whom they may have similar interests, therefore providing relational value

2. Providing valuable or interesting content that could range from a hot legal topic to a book group discussion

3. Allowing you to listen to group conversations to learn about needs, trends, professional current events

4. Meeting new people through encouraging invitees to bring a colleague with them to the event

5. Expanding relationships into a social/personal realm

6. Sharing hobbies and interests

7. Having fun

Periodically go through your WHOs, adjust whatever priority system you use to make a strategic selection of WHOs for focus and consider what form of modality will best fit your current goals for the relationship, provide value for the individual and accommodate the time available in your life for relationship development.

Chapter 18

Tracking Your HOWs—The Relationship Marathon™

How many HOWs should I do to get business development traction? Great question; hard and essential to answer. Early in the book we talked about business development as a behavior, and the two organizations that have outstanding track records in changing behavior are Weight Watchers and Alcoholics Anonymous. Among the features that make both programs so successful is counting core desired behaviors. As many of you know, AA counts the number of days a participant stays sober and rewards "days/years in" with coins. Weight Watchers motivates members daily through counting food and activity points. Wanting to build upon models that work for many people, I created the *Relationship Marathon*™ so you can numerically track your business development activities to measure your traction toward becoming a rainmaker.

The system is straightforward. It is built upon the Success Equation that we have talked about throughout the book:

A constantly growing WHOs List + sustained valuable contacts = increased business

Let me put this into "point system" language: you get points for increasing your number of WHOs and for HOWing, making contact with a connector or potential client from any of the four relationship buckets.

The Relationship Marathon™ challenges you to obtain 1,000 points in one year. This breaks down into:

- 84 points per month
- 21 points per week
- 4 points per day

The way you get points is straightforward:

1 point every time you add a new person or company to your WHOs List

1 point every time you make any type of contact with an individual

3 points for the first contact with an individual

Other ways to obtain points will be added over time, such as in the social media realm. Stay tuned to the Threshold Advisors blog (www.thresholdadvisors.com) for updates.

If the system seems easy, that's because it is. For example, you can get 4 points in a day by sending the same e-mail (with a personal introduction/greeting) to 4 different individuals; you can get 3 points by talking to one individual at a cocktail party you've never met before whom you deem to be a connector; you can get 20 points by identifying 20 ideal client companies through internet research. The system is designed to give you feedback about taking action and, in so doing, create relationship momentum.

The 1.0 version of the Marathon (due out in 2015) has some loopholes that I encourage you to close voluntarily: there is no system to assess the quality of your actions, so, if you are so disposed, you can talk briefly about a sports event to ten new people at a cocktail party, obtain no sense of whether they are connectors or ideal clients and ways to provide value to them, and award yourself 30 points. The *intention of the system* is to make all points of contact have value: that you keep FORD in mind during your point-generating cocktail party conversations; that the e-mails that you send to people offer substance, personal or professional, etc. In sum, award yourself points for HOWs (and adding WHOs) with a purpose in mind. Done with integrity, the Marathon will expand your relationships and keep your strategy moving forward.

In the near future, the Marathon will be utilizable online and through a smartphone app. For the time being I suggest that you manually calculate points daily on your calendar, in a specific section of a journal or in one of the columns on your WHOs List tracking form. When recording points, you will be best served by a short notation that describes the subject of the contact, including which F-O-R-D the contact addressed. Allocating points with notations of what you did to provide value will help you track activities and information that you are learning about the other person.

I am particularly excited about this system for firm lawyers, as it nicely parallels the way many of you track time: you know your hourly requirement, you make notations on a time sheet and therefore know where you stand with respect to firm (and perhaps your own) billable hour expectations.

I hope someday firms will use the Marathon to reward their lawyers for the enormous amount of effort required to bring in work, provide stellar client service and strengthen the firm's brand.

Chapter 19

The Art and Science of Social Media

By Guy Alvarez

The world of HOWs expanded with the invention of social media. The myriad of technology-based platforms provide creative, multidimensional, and, for many of us, totally perplexing ways to give value to individuals and groups and in so doing foster valuable, sustained relationships. Twenty-first-century legal business development requires that budding as well as seasoned rainmakers navigate the new vehicles both strategically and pragmatically. Guy Alvarez was introduced to me as "the social media guru in the legal space." I am thrilled to include wisdom and pointers from Guy in this book.

> **"If the world operates as one big market, every employee will compete with every person anywhere in the world who is capable of doing the same job. There are lots of them and many of them are hungry."**
> **Andy Grove**

We work in a global economy. The rapid evolution of technology has enabled the world to operate as one big market. Competition is fierce and many of the products and services that were unique at one point have become commodities. Technology is having an incredibly disruptive effect on business, all businesses, but particularly legal services.

There was a time when lawyers were able to merely focus on honing their craft. Partners or associates at a firm devoted themselves to practice without worrying about marketing or business development. Maybe one partner (who liked to drink) would be in charge of working the "old-boy network." But otherwise, most old-line law service firms discouraged young partners and associates from such mundane concerns as finding new clients, preferring that they focus their attention on taking care of existing accounts.

In the old days, business development simply meant another lunch at the club, or attending an occasional event where you could mingle over cocktails. Or if you were a real go-getter, you would give a talk at a seminar or conference that would let you highlight your expertise to a roomful of eager young professionals. But guess what? The old-boy network falls far short in today's hyper-connected, ultra-competitive world. The rules of business development have changed, even for the most established of firms. It is no longer enough to have gone to the right schools or to be a really good lawyer. In the hyper-connected world, a law firm must now engage with the rest of the business world through social media. Quite simply, that's where your clients and competitors are already living.

Consider for a moment the differences between the old-school and new-school approaches to business development and you'll quickly appreciate why the old tools and techniques are now so outdated:

Old-School Approach: If you're serious about working your connections the old-fashioned way, you'll stay busy attending a few events a week, pressing the flesh. But how many of the people you meet are really interested in what you do and how much opportunity do you have, with a brief handshake and introduction, to explain your expertise? And how does a brief personal meeting translate into a marketing opportunity so you'll be "top of mind" if a person you meet someday needs your services?

And don't forget the simple physical limits on the old-school approach of networking. How many events can you attend in a week? How much time and money will that cost you? Will it put a strain on your marriage or personal relationships if you're out night after night networking? And what if you are looking to network with people who live overseas? Are you going to travel all over the world attending cocktail parties and handing out business cards?

And even supposing you're prominent enough to get invited to speak at a conference, how many people will you reach on that given day? No matter how many events you speak at in the course of a year, they will never provide you a platform to reach a worldwide audience.

New-School Approach: Now consider the reach and engagement you can generate by actively participating in social media. With a well-crafted social media strategy, your message can be delivered to hundreds or even thousands of people—people with a known interest in your expertise—without leaving your desk.

Social media and social technologies enable lawyers to position themselves as thought leaders in their area of practice, develop a following and engage with a broader community online—all of which provides an opportunity to form meaningful trusted relationships with prospective clients, colleagues and influencers around the world. Instead of mingling at yet another Bar Association event, spend the time developing a micro-site, writing a weekly blog post and curating content on a daily basis. There is incredible power in the network. Once you establish your presence as a professional in social media, once you begin to share your expertise and point of view, social media provides enormous leverage for the time and energy you invest. The contacts you make begin to share your message with their personal networks, amplifying your reach, literally extending to people all over the world.

So that's the new paradigm for business development. The old-boy network is fast becoming an irrelevancy in light of the power and ubiquity of social media. This is a reality that all law firms can only ignore at their peril. So where do you begin? How do you go about building your personal brand on social media so that you can turn into the ultimate rainmaker?

It seems like a daunting task—particularly since you can anticipate the response from your firm's executive committee will most likely be that social media is nothing more than a passing business fad. Most law firms are incredibly resistant to change, painfully slow and deliberative in the approach to any innovation. And all too often a managing partner's first question is "What are our peer firms doing?" instead of considering whether a new idea makes sense.

The good news is that you don't need to get buy-in from your executive committee in order to get started. There are a few ways to begin experimenting and learning about social media that are more modest or experimental in fashion. It's all part of the journey.

The best place to start is LinkedIn, which bills itself as the networking site for professionals. Or you might think of it as Facebook for the corporate world. Started a decade ago, it already claims more than 220 million members worldwide, about a third of them in the U.S.

If you work at a large law firm, it's likely you already have a LinkedIn profile, as many firms upload staff bios to LinkedIn the same way they do to Martindale and West. But LinkedIn is much more than an online directory. It's definitely worth exploring in order to see how the business world is acclimating itself to social media.

Whether or not your firm has already uploaded a profile for you, it's a vital first step to create an updated profile that provides detailed information about your practice, interests and experience. I would also recommend injecting a personal touch or two into your listing to avoid making it too bland or formulaic. Of course, it's a good idea to check out how lawyers at other firms have presented themselves and it's worth reviewing listings for other professions.

Any lawyer who hopes to attract new clients, be known as a thought leader in their area of practice or benefit from their professional network ought to ensure that their LinkedIn profile is the best it can be. Success for a lawyer depends on conveying to prospects and clients that you're at the top of the practice area and LinkedIn can help you do that. The first and most important step is to ensure that your profile is optimized and filled out completely.

Lawyers with complete profiles are forty times more likely to be noticed through LinkedIn than a lawyer with an incomplete one. Complete profiles rank higher in LinkedIn's search results. LinkedIn wants to make sure its results are accurate, so they promote profiles that are filled out before they display incomplete profiles. Taking the time to complete your profile shows LinkedIn that your profile deserves to rank higher.

One way to ensure that your profile is complete is to look at the profile strength meter on the right side of your profile. The more information you add, the more powerful, robust and complete your profile is.

Here are some tips to help you reach All-Star status:

1. Update your photo. It should be recent, professional and represent you or your firm.

2. The headline (a.k.a. the most crucial 120 characters on your profile) should stand out, include important key words that are specific to your practice area and make people want to read more about you.

3. Write your summary in a tone you would use to address clients over coffee. Your description should make them want to hire you.

4. Make sure your background and work experience are relevant to your current practice. The most important information should be at the top. Don't just regurgitate your résumé. Take advantage of the chance to expand on topics that don't fit on an 8.5 x 11-inch piece of paper.

5. Provide specific instructions for potential clients to learn more about you and your firm. Share specific links or documents that will help them contact you.

6. Join groups. There are so many groups related to law on LinkedIn for you to choose from. These give you the chance to increase your relevancy, find new people and send direct messages to thousands of people who aren't in your network. Definitely get involved in a group where your clients are likely to be and contribute to discussions.

7. Connect with all of your clients. They are your best source of referrals, so reach out and thank them!

8. Share a status update every day. This is an easy opportunity to share relevant information, demonstrate your experience in your field and stay prominent in your network.

9. Use the alumni search feature to expand your network. You can connect with your colleagues from law school or roommates from college and make new connections.

10. Use the new publishing feature on LinkedIn. This is especially useful if you or your firm doesn't currently have a blog, because it will enable you to demonstrate your knowledge and analysis on substantive issues of law that pertain to your practice.

Experiment and take advantage of all of the features on LinkedIn. You can share a portfolio, list publications you've written for and even mention your volunteer experience. Your coworkers and potential clients notice these things, and that could make all the difference.

With your profile complete, the next step is to start adding people to your network. LinkedIn makes this easy by allowing you to enter your email contact list and then identifying which of your contacts are already on LinkedIn. Another way to do this is by entering your college, law school or employment information; here again LinkedIn will provide you with information about members of your network already on LinkedIn.

Once you establish your personal network, you should spend time exploring LinkedIn groups. There are thousands of them, many with sizable and very active memberships, including a number of them devoted to legal practice areas. However, don't just join groups for lawyers. Remember one of LinkedIn's greatest strengths is that its membership is drawn from across the business world, so this is a great chance to see and be seen as a member of non-legal groups that relate to your practice as well. As an M&A lawyer, you may find it useful to join a group devoted to the telecom or energy industry. Or a tort litigator might be interested to join a pharmaceutical industry group. Some groups you will be able to join right away, others require the acceptance of the group owner.

As a group member, you'll be able to monitor questions or topics posted by other members and read through the discussion threads spawned by those questions. Most groups will notify you via e-mail when there are new discussions or new comments on older discussions. Here is where you can start to make your mark in the social world. Look for opportunities to demonstrate your knowledge and experience. If you see people posting questions or starting discussions where you have something valuable to add, then by all means do so. Here is your opportunity to start building relationships and establishing yourself as a thought leader in your field.

But remember, particularly when posting comments in a LinkedIn non-legal forum, you want to avoid any risk of creating an inadvertent client relationship. (Most firms automatically append a disclaimer to the footer of email messages, but this will not be included when you post a message into a LinkedIn group.) So it's important to look carefully at your jurisdiction's applicable rules to see how they affect participation on LinkedIn and other social networking sites. Many jurisdictions do require disclaimers, and if your jurisdiction is one of them, you must include it. It may also be a good practice for lawyers to include some form of disclaimer on their LinkedIn profile.

Once you have contributed to other people's discussions and you feel comfortable with the style of the group, then, and only then, should you start posting your own content or starting your own discussions.

The next step is to think beyond LinkedIn. Most lawyers who have taken steps to build their brand on social media have the mistaken belief that all you have to do is to participate on LinkedIn. This is a mistake. Lawyers need to think beyond this single platform when it comes to their social and digital strategies. Lawyers need to leverage all social networks in order to reach their target audience. The challenge is figuring out the right networks to use for each particular effort. For example, if a lawyer is interested in reaching international clients, then leveraging the size and power of Google+ or the reach of Twitter likely provides a more effective solution than LinkedIn.

The fact is that there are fewer lawyers using Google+ than are on LinkedIn. Google+ is the second largest social network, and similar to LinkedIn it has thousands of thriving communities (the equivalent of groups on LinkedIn). Therefore the ability for a lawyer's content to stand out and be noticed by prospects and clients may be significantly better on Google+.

It's also worth bearing in mind that reporters and the media constantly monitor Twitter for ideas and trends. They look for interesting content and frequently contact lawyers who they deem have specific knowledge or expertise in a particular subject area or industry trend. If a lawyer is looking to have exposure through traditional media channels and develop press relations, then it becomes critical for them to deploy a Twitter strategy to develop a following amongst reporters and influencers.

Since its founding in 2006, Twitter has mushroomed into one of the most active sites on the Internet, boasting more than 500 million registered users, who collectively post more than 340 million tweets a day.

For those of us reared in a world of broadcast media, Twitter represents a fundamental and somewhat bewildering change in the mode of communication. It is a self-organizing and decentralized network that consists of individual broadcasters and their followers. Followers, in turn, may be broadcasters on their own, so an interesting tweet will often be rebroadcast (or retweeted) by the initial recipient and thus information propagates rapidly across the network precisely because of its decentralized nature. This is part of the reason Twitter has proved to be an invaluable tool for social activists, including the highly visible role it played in support of the Arab Spring movements. Dictators can seize control of the TV station, but it's much more difficult to silence the Twitter-sphere.

But to be honest, it's not everyone's cup of tea, and it's really only well suited to certain types of messaging. All tweets being subject to a strict 140-character limit, brevity is the key driver of Twitter's success, but also inherently limits the network's suitability to information that can be successfully packaged in short bursts. For most lawyers, accustomed as we are to endless footnoting and qualifying clauses, this may seem like a crippling constraint.

Perhaps it's most helpful to think of Twitter as a powerful tool for quickly monitoring and gathering information—whether on clients, prospects, competitors or influencers. Twitter can also serve as a sort of daily alert service where you can track the latest developments within your practice area and follow the people and sources that regularly publish updated content.

In order to get started, you should set up your own Twitter account—this is useful even if you don't intend to originate tweets yourself. Make sure it looks professional. Once your account is set up, you're ready to begin searching for people you know or influencers in your space. You can search for companies or individuals or you can keyword search for tweets that relate to topics of interest. Once you find a Twitter source of interest, you simply sign up as a follower.

If you sign up to follow a number of feeds, you will also likely find it helpful to build one or more Twitter lists in order to avoid being inundated by all the messages. Twitter lists enable you to segment feeds by category. You can create a Twitter list that pulls together feeds on M&A, the telco industry or any other topic of interest in your practice.

Hashtags are another important feature of Twitter that people use to categorize posts by keyword:

- People insert the hashtag symbol (#) before a relevant keyword or phrase (no spaces) in their post to categorize those posts.
- If you post a message with a hashtag on Twitter, anyone who does a search for that hashtag may find your post.
- Clicking on a hashtagged word in any message will return a list of other tweets marked with that keyword.
- Hashtags can occur anywhere in a post—at the beginning, middle, or end.
- Hashtagged words that become very popular will often be highlighted as Trending Topics.

Particularly if you're using Twitter for promotional purposes, it's important to use hashtags effectively since they can help make messages much more visible on the network. Here are a few additional tips for using hashtags correctly:

- Don't #spam #with #hashtags. Don't over-tag a single post.

- Best practices recommend using no more than two hashtags per post.

- Use hashtags only on posts relevant to the topic.

Although the 140-character limit renders Twitter inappropriate for long, substantive messages, Twitter has proven to be extremely effective as a marketing and business development tool. For a lawyer who is creating and publishing valuable content on a firm website or blog, Twitter provides the most cost-effective solution for driving traffic to that content. It gives you an easy tool to extend your reach across Twitter's pool of 500 million users. This will work most effectively with valuable content that can then be promoted through tweets that make effective use of hashtags. This way your promotional messages will be visible to your pre-existing followers as well as to users who are reading and searching on those hashtagged keywords. And anyone who finds your post to be of value may retweet it to his or her followers and so on, extending your reach across the network.

For active users, Twitter has also proved to be a very good tool for developing relationships with influencers and others who share your interests and concerns. These relationships typically develop as a result of the way information is shared or passed on over the network. This sharing—more formally called curation or curating third-party content—is an important part of the ethos of social media. After you find people who are influencers or frequent writers on your area of interest, you may decide to retweet or mention their posts in messages to your own followers. There are two benefits to this:

1. You are providing something useful to your followers —content that you believe is informative and of high quality—which thus enhances your value as an information provider.

2. This gives you the opportunity to develop a relationship with those people whose content you curate and share. Thanks to the sharing ethos of social media, this may prove especially helpful if they are influencers in your area and have large followings. When you share their content and mention them (engaging with them), they will be more likely to share your content and mention

you when you have something valuable to add, which enables you, over time, to reach a larger audience.

Most law firms and lawyers don't have a clue how to use Twitter effectively. They typically use it for promotional messaging or simply as a platform for distributing press releases. This type of promotional content is not well received by readers and provides almost no possibility for meaningful engagement or sharing of content.

Twitter is unlike most other distribution channels. In order to create true engagement, lawyers should focus on creating valuable and worthwhile content that educates the reader or provides them with meaningful, actionable information. Legal analysis, white papers, interviews, tips, videos, infographics: these are all examples of content strategies that work, no matter what the size constraints of Twitter may be. Once you have something valuable to share, the key then is to write a clever and engaging post in 140 characters or less.

After experimenting with LinkedIn and Twitter, the next step is for the rainmaker to create a blog or microsite.

Blogs—an abbreviation for web logs—actually predate the advent of social media and have been commonplace on the web for well over a decade. By providing a simple and standardized suite of authoring tools, a blog enables any individual or organization to quickly start publishing content online. You can literally set up your own blog in less than five minutes using one of the common platforms like WordPress or Blogger. And it won't cost you anything to get started.

Before you set up your blog, however, I strongly recommend you take a look around to see what other lawyers are doing. Given the low cost and ease of use, legal blogs have proliferated over the last few years. There are thousands of them out there on a wide variety of topics, some with extensive legal commentary, some more personal in flavor, from solo practitioners, mid-sized firms and practice groups at the largest firms.

You can get a quick idea of the extensive range of blog resources from The Blawg Directory compiled by The ABA Journal that currently lists more than 3,600 law blogs, organized in dozens of categories. If that sounds overwhelming, the ABA also runs an annual competition where it selects the top 100 legal blogs called the Blawg 100.

Or if you prefer, you can create your own customized blog clipping service. After you find blogs with content of interest to you, there are a few tools you can use that will make it easier to manage what admittedly can be an overwhelming flow of content.

The software tools I would recommend are Feedly or Flipboard, each of which is easy to use and enables you to subscribe to multiple blogs, view them in a single page and then organize the content in accordance with your own preferences.

After you have had a chance to examine and read blogs from other lawyers, it is time to start creating content. This is the most important part of a lawyer's social media strategy. You have to determine and find content that is valuable to your target audience. Coming up with ideas or topics for your blog is critical if you want to succeed. There are a couple basic categories that legal blog posts generally fall into:

1. **Generic practice pointers/ checklists, etc.** This is often a staple of legal blogging. Though these items can be bland and hard to present in narrative form, they nonetheless help drive an important marketing objective, helping collect e-mail addresses from readers who want to download the full item. Examples of these sorts of blog posts include checklists such as: ten pointers to consider as you prepare for your securities filing or corporate tax return; five tips on how to maintain your corporate records in good order; what is your company's e-mail retention policy; etc. The place to start is to look through your files and see what kind of generic advice pieces you have on hand. If you don't have this sort of material already available, then you should think about putting a few items together.

2. **Client stories.** Ideally these stories should involve a specific situation or problem and illustrate your approach to handling it. Names and details will often need to be changed or omitted to avoid disclosing client confidences, but the stories should include enough specificity to be real and convincing. The best story items are those that illustrate a specific issue or practice problem. For example, consider how to tell a short story about the importance of building client confidence. It's hard to effectively represent a client if they don't tell you what's really going on. Still, some clients are hesitant or reluctant to share information that they think will give you a bad impression of them or their business. But how can you defend them in a deposition or help in a negotiation if you don't really know the details of what's going on? So, do you have a story about a client who was reluctant to share a critical piece of information with you?

3. **Reacting to recent legal developments.** This is a very important staple of all legal blogging: reacting to new developments. In the legal world, there are new releases from the SEC and IRS every day. There are interesting cases that get

decided or lawsuits that get filed. Any of these items may present an opportunity for a new blog story. The important thing is to be set up with a procedure to track new developments and then come up with your own twist or explanation of why it's important for people to know about it. For example, as I write this I find that on the SEC website this morning is an important news item. Here is the headline: "SEC Warns Investors about Marijuana." This is an eye-catching headline and an issue of potential significance in the micro-cap world. It could make for a lively and entertaining short blog post. To be relevant, a blog topic doesn't need to be ripped straight from "today's" headlines. Although this release from the SEC is dated May 16th, you could publish an item about this any time in the next sixty days and it would still be pertinent and timely.

4. **Personal stories that relate to your life as a lawyer.** There are a number of things you do in the course of your daily life that might provide grist for a blog post. Maybe you sit on the board of a non-profit agency or are active in a section or committee of your local bar. Or maybe you're reading an interesting book or magazine article that touches on a current legal issue. These sorts of items can be turned into interesting blog posts, but it's always important to tie the conversation back to an issue or problem that relates to your legal practice. Always try to make it relevant and useful to your clients and prospects.

Remember that variety is important to retain the interest of readers over the long haul. The best blogs do not stick to a single formula or approach, but try to provide readers with a mix of content. I strongly recommend that our clients utilize more than a single approach in order to keep their blogs lively.

Making it rain by using social media takes time, patience and dedication. You have to think about your target audience and then develop a steady stream of valuable and engaging content. Lawyers expecting to be able to land clients overnight by using social media will be sorely disappointed. In the real world it takes time and effort to build trust with a prospective client. Social media is no different, but if used properly and with authenticity, it can be a marvelous source of new and repeat business over the course of time.

Guy, a former attorney, is the Chief Engagement Officer at Good2bSocial, LLC, a consulting company that helps law firms and professionals in the legal industry understand how to use social media to delight their customers, engage with their prospects and enable their employees to become more productive and innovative. Guy can be reached at Guy@good2bsocial.com or you can follow him on Twitter at @guylaw1313. You can also follow his blog posts on the Good2bSocial website, http://good2bsocial.com.

Part IV

Tools, Systems, Processes

How do you get your substantive work done? Do you do it on the fly? By yourself with no assistance from anyone? Keep all of your records in your head? Talk to clients when you feel like it? Bill time based on how long it "felt like" it took you? (Some of you may have silently said "yes" to this last one.) Similar to the way excellent client work is conducted, the ongoing use of well-crafted tools, systems and processes will streamline, facilitate and organize your business development efforts.

Chapter 20

Your Business Development Blueprint

When we really don't want to do something, we tend to relegate it to "I'll do it when I can" status, which typically means taking spontaneous, random action when you feel like it. This stance pretty well describes what I have found to be most lawyers' attitudes about business development. As a result they have no *real* plan; clear short-term, mid-range or long-term objectives; or even a "business development to-do list." Most law firms require their lawyers to submit a business plan at different points in their careers, sometimes even annually, but most lawyers I know consider this exercise annoying and spend little time filling out the template in a meaningful way.

Just as you construct a plan to foster success for your clients, in order to move toward your own goals, you must have one for yourself.

The Business Development Blueprint is your MACRO plan, a big-picture overview of your direction. I like it better than many firm business plans, as it is very specific, short and captures useable information about your practice area and industry focus while also asking about issues that will impact taking action, including challenges and opportunities, resources, ways to maintain momentum and goals. A template of the Business Development Blueprint appears in Appendix B. Let me go briefly through each of the eight questions to explain the intention of each item so that you can adjust each one to best fit your needs.

Summarize your business development focus going forward.

> This is a very brief, few-word overview of your direction: "Medical devices, particularly prosthetic arena." (NOTE there are no "HOWs" in this segment, just a response to where your focus will lie.)

What do you see as the "hot topic" or topics in your practice area today and over the near term?

This question prepares you for conversations and for proactive action by asking you to think about what issues make your legal practice most relevant over the next year to all businesses (not just your industry niche). For example, has there been a new regulation, law or decision that impacts the way businesses strategize? Are there new trends in the way companies conduct business, new technologies that impact legal positioning, new ideas all within your practice area? These hot topics may be great sources of ways to expand business with existing firm clients; therefore, keep your colleagues abreast of these issues.

In this space make a list of the topics, just using three or four words per topic.

What do you see as the hot topic or topics in your niche or major area of industry focus today and in the near term?

This question focuses on your industry niche. While the previous question was practice-area-specific, this question prompts you to think about ALL issues, legal and nonlegal, that impact businesses in your niche. The more expansive your thinking, the more interesting your conversations will be and the more capable you will be to assist in a valuable capacity. This may take some important research if you have not lived in the niche for an extended period of time.

In this space make a list of a few topics you will explore with WHOs in this niche.

What do you see as the most significant challenges to your business development success over the next twelve months?

This question focuses on YOU by asking you to identify potential blocks to making rain. These elements might be motivational, personal or related to the firm, the economy, demands on your time, lack of resources, etc. Thinking proactively about impediments or potential impediments propels you to consider solutions. You might even decide to scale back your business development goals for this year, yet commit to accelerating the following year or gear your activities in a direction that may be more feasible to do during a challenging period in your life or career such as a trial or family issue. Anticipate difficulties, plan accordingly and keep taking business development action.

What do you see as the most significant opportunities for your business development success over the next twelve months?

I don't know about you, but I would much rather think about potential opportunities than challenges. This question nudges you to think outside the box about up-and-coming directions for your clients, potential clients and ideal clients. Are there changes in the legal marketplace, ways to communicate with people, new organizations to join, new issues to address that you can position yourself as "the first" to discuss, or have you started a relationship with a new connector? Be gutsy with your ideas—try them out—they may or may not work, that's okay. Recognizing opportunities is among the best antidotes for feeling stuck and pessimistic about your business development direction. Recording these ideas on your Blueprint gives you a reference point when you are ready to initiate new directions and/or conversations.

What is your plan for maintaining business development momentum from the past several months?

It is essential that you take consistent action "no matter what." (Have I stated this too often?) This question reminds you to have a plan and stick to it. It might also trigger you to evaluate what you have done over the past several months that has spurred consistent action (so keep doing that!) or prompt you to identify times you have abandoned your resolve and think about ways to avoid those pitfalls in the future. I see this question as a recommitment to take action in whatever ways are best for you at this point in time. You might note that you will work with a business development buddy every Friday or that you will have monthly meetings with someone from the business development department.

What resources (not time) could best support your business efforts?

Here is the question I ask myself to think expansively about this item: if time and money were not an issue, what would I use to move myself forward? First, answer big, as if you won the lottery. This fosters creativity. Would you want a business development professional dedicated only to you? Would you hire a research team, wave a magic wand and, presto, have a list of ideal clients? What are the ultimate resources that you believe you need to succeed? With a grand list of necessary resources, albeit defined in glorious magnitude, ask yourself: "In what way CAN I bring these resources into my life?" Talk to your "team" and see how they can help you compile what you need.

By this time next year I will have ...

And finally, your goals and commitment to the goals. Be very specific. Here are some examples:

- I will have started my WHOs List
- I will have contacted four people per week
- I will have expanded my relationships with a, b, c
- I will have brought my assistant into my business development activities
- I will have attended x, y, z trade associations

Make sure your goals are achievements that you can control. You can't control whether a given company gives you a piece of business. You CAN control whether and how you position yourself for the business.

This Blueprint was designed to be a *tool*, something that is easily at your disposal and used frequently. Therefore, I strongly recommend that you:

1. Keep it to one page only by writing brief, easy-to-see-at-a-glance notes that contain key words, not full sentences

2. Print it out on colored paper so that it doesn't get lost among all of the papers on your desk

3. Post (or place) it somewhere that you are likely to see often

Use the Blueprint to maintain strong awareness about the importance of business development in your career. Let it be a tool that keeps business development from becoming an "out of sight, out of mind" element in your life. Your answers to the eight sections (that is way fewer than most business development plans) are intended to remind you about your direction when you need clarity. This is your guide, the answer to the question, "What are you doing with respect to business development?"

Update the Blueprint at least annually, especially the hot topics. Reminding yourself about the hot topics keeps you relevant to your relationships and allows you to have proactive conversations about current trends and potential important occurrences that may impact people and businesses around you.

Chapter 21

WHOs List (a Review)

We have discussed the form and function of the WHOs List throughout this book. Where the Blueprint is a macro tool, the WHOs List is a micro tool: it is an Excel spreadsheet that lists all of the relationships that you have and want to have in the future and therefore very specifically spells out WHO will help you develop business (clients and connectors), and, should you so choose, can record brief notes about HOW (and when) you will initiate and sustain the relationships. It is the embodiment of the core strategy for rainmaking: The more WHOs you have and the more valuable connections you have with the WHOs, the higher your likelihood of success.

Your WHOs List contains relationships from all four Relationship Buckets: Inside the Firm, Past and Current Clients, Personal/Professional Network, Industry/Geography Niche (when relevant). It can function as a tracking tool to record your points of contact and can be a record of when you want to schedule the next point of connection with each WHO.

Your WHOs List is an evolving document; add to it throughout your career. Your style determines whether your list is electronic or on paper, and your work style will determine specific nuances about how you use your list: some people organize it by relationship bucket, some people utilize a priority system of organization, some people color-code elements. As with all tools, experiment and adjust to discover the most effective way to put this tool to use.

Chapter 22

Notes and Records

Throughout the discussions so far in this book I am sure you have been impressed by the enormous amount of information about individuals and companies that must be acquired by a successful rainmaker. While the FORD system of gathering information, asking questions and providing value tells you what to *learn* about people, it is essential that you *record* this information so that you can use it easily. Making a file about each person with whom you are developing a relationship, like a doctor does with each patient, keeps your information readily available and organized. Another system, less easy to use, is a daily journal in which to record information you learn about people as you acquire it. The good news with this journal system is that you wrote the information down; the challenging news is that the information is hard to find when you need it, as it is stored by date, not by name. Find a system that works for you that gathers information in a format that makes the information accessible and useable.

Jotting notes is not an *exercise,* it is a technique that enables you to utilize and leverage important information to relate to people fully and personally. Some people ask me, "Isn't it disingenuous to refer to notes before forging relationships? After all, if someone is important to you, shouldn't you be able to speak to them spontaneously?" These questions reflect an unfair expectation of yourself. You review notes before client meetings, don't you? Doctors certainly look at your chart before conducting your examination. You bring a list to the supermarket, right? Notes allow you to store and use information of all kinds that is important to you. There is absolutely no shame in checking your notes to recall the name of the college from which a key contact graduated or challenges that he shared with you. Great relationships can be developed by caring enough to take the time to write notes. Use all the knowledge you can accumulate through research and conversation as relationship building blocks. Actively USING this information SHOWS people that you care. Being a caring individual (or firm) is not just a statement on your bio or website.

Chapter 23

Business Development Diary/Journal

I don't know about you, but I come up with great ideas for business development at the most awkward times: in the shower, while I am driving, while attending lectures, etc. A business development diary is a valuable tool to help you capture your brilliant ideas such as creative actions to take, people to contact and ways to provide value to others. Some of the lawyers with whom I work have the diary divided into sections such as notes from coach, immediate to-dos, ideas and information about people (to be transcribed into the appropriate relationship file).

Another very important segment for the diary/journal is to house your vision and goals. As you grow and develop *and* as you become more successful, it is likely that your vision about what CAN BE will expand. That is a wonderful occurrence. You may realize that your vision for a five million-dollar-book of business was conservative and you are ready to push it out to seven million. You may be inspired to create a larger network of relationships as you see how one person is connected to another. Drawing a map or flow chart in your journal may concretize your thinking. A dream idea for retirement or even for right now may develop as you work with a particular company, meet a fascinating person or even watch a thought-provoking television show. Write it down and start to think about what has to happen in order to obtain your dream job. Another one of my favorite books is *Write It Down Make It Happen*, by Henriette Anne Klauser. Her research discovered that individuals who write down their goals and visions have a higher likelihood of making them happen than those who keep their great ideas in their minds.

Your diary/journal can be among the most potent of your tools. Buy one, make one, set one up on your computer (although I favor the old-fashion paper kind) and use it as a mechanism to capture important ideas and directions.

What I most want to impress upon you is the importance of recording all information related to business development. Don't allow this essential part of your career to be something that you "just keep in your head." The notes that you keep are reviewable and allow you to refer to important information that you received from prior conversations. When I see someone I haven't seen in a long time, mention something that is central to them and they gleefully respond, "I can't believe you remembered that!" I know that my note taking and keeping efforts paid off!

Chapter 24

Calendar

Your calendar is your best friend for keeping you organized and moving forward. Use only ONE calendar, be it paper or electronic so that you don't get caught putting items and events in different places and then missing something important. Use your calendar to schedule time with yourself for business development thinking, planning and researching just as you do meetings with others. Conceptualize each small goal/activity as a "client" and make an appointment in your calendar to do it. Most lawyers with whom I work report that the first or last part of the day is the best time to "schedule appointments" with themselves. Warning: canceling on yourself is a bad habit to begin. Business is critical to your goals; as you reserve a time, renew your business development commitment to yourself.

Another great use of the calendar is as a mechanism to remind you to be in touch with specific people, especially on a continuing basis. Make a list of those WHOs that you want to be in touch with frequently. How often would you like to make contact with each person? For example, Person A you want to be in touch with every other month, Person B you want to be in touch with quarterly, Person C you want to contact twice per year, etc. Have your assistant, or yourself, schedule these "touches" into your calendar as repeating meetings. At the assigned time, an "appointment" will appear on your electronic calendar reminding you that it is time to connect. If you are paper-based, when you decide that you want to be in touch with a certain individual frequently, place notes to yourself at the appropriate time throughout the year.

Finally, at the beginning or end of the year, schedule a day to look backwards and forwards. At these meetings ask yourself questions such as:

1. What relationships did I deepen? How did I do this?

2. What do I want to do differently in the upcoming year with respect to relationships?

3. Where do I want to focus most of my efforts in the upcoming years?

4. WHO do I want to meet? WHO do I want to know better?

5. What progress have I made toward my goals?

Also, at your private annual meeting, review and update your Blueprint. Set annual goals. Create activities to support those goals. Congratulate yourself for all you did and commit to doing whatever it takes to move even further toward what is important to you.

Chapter 25

Your Personal Business Development Team

Do you feel alone as you pursue business and relationships with too much to do and not enough time to do it all? Many lawyers experience that attending to everything in this book (and other tips they have learned from business development experts) is impossible as there is not enough time in the day to do the research and planning, let alone relationship development. Not knowing how to do it all blocks many of you. The good news is that pulling together a team to advance toward your goals, whether you are practicing solo or in a large firm, is at your disposal—you just need to know what you need and how to state your "asks" clearly so that people who can help you give you exactly what you want. Let's look at some tasks that you need done and then explore who can help you.

1. Identify and research companies in your niche

2. Research key people across all relationship buckets

3. Gather, record and consolidate information about WHOs, such as contact info, bios, areas of responsibility, etc.

4. Stay abreast of news concerning individuals and companies on WHOs List

5. Seek out events, trade associations, seminars, conferences for membership, speaking, writing and attending

6. Maintain schedule for next point of communication to assure ongoing communication with key people

7. Track development of relationships by recording when contact occurs

8. Stay abreast of hot topics in your practice area

9. Broadly expand points of contact in ideal client companies

10. Find connectors

11. Keep all public biographical information current

12. Post in social media outlets

Firms provide an array of professional resources. Of course, their existence and even availability to you (which may differ depending on your status in the firm) will vary. Here are some professionals that are potentially very valuable to you. See if they are at your office:

Your Assistant: Many assistants are delighted to expand their role and activities to include being a "relationship manager," especially if you invite innovative thinking and independent action into the description of the responsibilities. First, explain the nature of business development and role(s) he/she could take in helping you. It would be beneficial to have them read this book so they understand your direction and activities that could be helpful. People are most engaged when they come up with ideas as opposed to being *told* what to do; therefore, begin by asking what ideas he/she might have to advance your business development goals and ways that he/she would like to be involved. Go over the above task list, and together, think about a sequence of activities that will move you forward, such as first putting together your WHOs List and then researching information about top-priority WHOs. Several attorneys with whom I work have weekly business development meetings with their assistant. They have asked their assistant to write down activities that the attorney agrees to do in the week ahead, hold them accountable (gently) to take action and frequently ask them how they are doing with the assigned tasks. Having an essential role on a team, as opposed to "just answering the phone," fosters excellent work products, happy people and the increased likelihood that *your* goals and success will become *shared* goals and success.

Firm Librarian: There are probably no better researchers than librarians, especially ones trained to assist lawyers. Their breadth of knowledge and access to resources that contain valuable information can be instrumental to your success. Set a time to explain to the librarian what kinds of information you need and ask for support. The more succinct you are about what you need, the higher the likelihood is that you will get what you need. For example, if you are researching the largest companies in the nuclear power industry in the United States (or the world), state exactly that. If you need the names of midsized pharmaceutical companies in the northeastern United States, provide the parameters of what "midsize" and "northeastern" mean to you. As mentioned above, when people experience themselves to be a valuable and appreciated part of your team, they tend to work hard, be an advocate for you and enjoy the tasks. If you don't have access to a firm librarian, consider seeking one out at a law school or a public library or even hiring a research assistant. Delegating research allows you to use your time to focus on the actual tasks involved with developing sustained relationships. It also increases the quality of the information you receive, as it places this large task in the hands of a research expert.

Business Development/Marketing Professionals: In my opinion, the individuals who carry the weight of driving the message about your firm on their shoulders are among the unsung heroes of a law firm. I constantly admire the immense juggling act in which they are engaged across a huge breadth of activities including public relations, research, answering RFPs, website content maintenance, presentation preparation, event planning and so much more. They are strategists, resources, coaches and advocates. Appreciate them, access them and include them as invaluable parts of your business development team. Your first step in engaging them is learning about their capabilities, resources, expertise and time availability. Given the importance law firms place on generating business, it is ironic that most business development departments are understaffed. Some business development/marketing departments don't even have highly trained experts, and others do not give their well-trained professionals time and *permission* to think and act strategically. Talk to the people assigned to attend to business development in your firm. Share your goals and ask them about their time and ability to assist. Minimally, they can inform you about systems that the firm has set up to support business development and internal connections. They can also be instrumental voices of support, stopping by your office to make sure you are taking the actions you have committed to yourself, spreading the word about your accomplishments and connecting you with others inside the firm with whom you can collaborate to develop relationships with WHOs similar to yours. Whether these important people have been hired to lead strategic efforts or only keep the website up-to-date, they have access to ideas and relationships that can help you thrive. In addition, they know about the systems the firm has purchased to help you. Ask them for a briefing about resources, including client relationship management systems (CRM), Knowledge Information Systems, public relations support and tools. Considering them as instrumental members of your team makes smart sense.

Colleagues: As I've heard it told, law firms began when two lawyers decided to share office space. They worked independently, focusing on their own work and their own income. That model expanded to firms with thousands of lawyers spread over many offices all over the globe, and now the tradition of attorneys working independently is alive and well in a majority of firms. The legal marketplace is so vast with multiple points of entry into potential client organizations, broad-reaching and complex needs of buyers and an abundance of "good enough" lawyers vying for business that it is extremely difficult for individuals, acting alone, without colleagues and connections, to obtain business. Collaborating with colleagues to combine goals, WHOs and efforts is more efficient than solo rainmaking.

I am aware that there are many structural challenges to collaborative business development in law firms, not the least of which is that the compensation system of many firms often spurs internal competition and relationship hoarding. I am choosing to put that reality aside for the moment to highlight the benefits and methodology of collegial collaboration.

Being engaged by a firm as an outside coach tasked to work with twelve to sixteen individuals often has a side benefit for an organization: through possessing detailed knowledge about individual business development directions, I often discover similar interests, WHOs and directions among those with whom I work. This is especially true across practice areas. For example, three of us from Threshold Advisors worked with sixteen litigators for six months. We helped them develop strategies, including selecting an industry niche. Through the coaching process we discovered that three out of the sixteen had extensive experience with different aspects of the food industry. Despite the fact that all of these partners worked out of the same office and crossed paths frequently, they did not know about their similar clientele. Bringing them together fostered a discussion about ways they, together, could become known in the industry, be responsive to the different needs of the clients they already knew and share the work of staying abreast of industry trends. Subsequently, they brought other lawyers into their group, now meet regularly and are bringing work into the firm based on their collective expertise and shared relationships.

Practice group leaders that implement a collaborative strategy will expand the business development pie of the group as a whole. Several initial steps are essential to success, such as defining a vision for the group; researching the individual practices of all partners to determine industry foci and relationships that can be leveraged; assessing the business development strengths and weakness of all group members at all levels of expertise; and, finally, crafting a strategy that will engage all members, raise the group profile, expand organizational and individual relationships and ultimately, *over time,* lead to success. In this model, frequent meetings and communication are essential. Decisions developed through discussion, regular gatherings to share information, shared visions that may require sacrificing individual directions are issues that possess multiple challenges. However, the opportunities born of combining relationships, resources and expertise are exponential. Such collaboration fosters a model that mirrors the interconnected, networked, global world in which business is currently conducted, and thereby can facilitate growing and sustaining relationships among individuals and entities.

Family: Without a doubt, the most important part of my team is my significant other, John. John is not a lawyer. He worked for numerous large companies within one industry in product development and sales, rising up the corporate ladder for about forty years until he started his own company about seven years ago. Every day we discuss our challenges and opportunities. We coach each other to find novel solutions when none seem available and push each other when progress seems slow, such as my stalling to write this book. Despite being in very different lines of work, and not truly understanding the intricacies of what each other does, we know enough to make introductions and connections. For example, one day I was at a sports bar in Connecticut, the only place I could watch my favorite football team, the Washington Redskins. During a commercial I chatted with a young man sitting next to me and discovered that his work involved manufacturing plastic molds. Knowing that this was an element of John's work, I called John on my cell phone and made an introduction. They set a time to speak later that week.

John is on the search for connections for me as well. He's always finding me articles about my clients that I can then, in turn, share with my clients. Several times he has even met with a client who wanted to develop a niche within his industry. He is a role model, clear thinker and spirited cheerleader. Plus, he makes sure that I don't take myself too seriously. Knowing that we speak throughout the day and that he will ask, "How's it going?" keeps me accountable to do what I say I am going to do. And, since he knows me better than most everyone else, he knows what to say when I am down and how to give me gentle yet direct feedback when I don't make sense. Integrating heart and business might be tricky for some people. For me, it intertwines the aspects of my life and delightfully expands the bounds of this important relationship.

The role of a significant other doesn't have to be as extensive as mine is. Minimally, keep your partner or close friend apprised of your strategic thinking when you attend an event. Tell them whom you want to meet and why and how they can help you find and forge these connections. If they are not a part of your industry, prepare them for conversations that might take place so they can participate.

Making individuals close to you instrumental parts of your business development team can be instrumental AND fun. You pursue success, celebrate wins and have compelling strategy meetings together. A few hints about having family and close friends as a part of your team: make sure you clearly communicate what you want and need, don't expect them to be mind readers, be clear about who you would like to meet and make sure you know what they need and position yourself to give in kind.

A few other individuals you may not have thought about can also lend important assistance:

Virtual Assistant: This is a relatively new profession that can expand any and all of your capabilities. Virtual Assistants are professionals who provide help from a distance, not onsite (although under some circumstances some can arrange face-to-face meetings). The skill set of these professionals varies with each person: travel arrangements, purchasing gifts, managing social media and marketing campaigns, editing, traditional administration and more. Typically they work on an hourly basis; some via a prearranged package of time. If you are a part of a large law firm, these professionals can help you privately (and confidentially) for short or long periods of time. To learn more, contact the International Virtual Assistant Association (IVAA) at www.IVAA.org.

Research Assistants: These days research seems to be the purview of the young; they know how to powerfully use the Internet to track down all kinds of "hidden treasures" such as information about clients, names of potential clients inside your niche, events within industries, etc. If you do not have access to a business development professional inside your firm, want to pursue your goals quietly or your firm doesn't have such a department, call in the "professional" researchers: law students, summer associates and college students. Access to these young adults will vary; however, using these relatively inexpensive individuals can go a long way toward accumulating the information you need to create in-depth valuable relationships.

Part V

Taking Action—Creating Momentum YOUR Way

How many times have you read a book, become inspired, even excited and determined, and left that book sitting on your desk or nightstand never to be touched again? The best intentions, right? As this book approaches the finish line, I want to do everything I can to take the content that you have so patiently pored through and put it into action—YOUR Action, YOUR Way.

Chapter 26

Questions to Help You Begin and Focus

Many psychologists speak about the concept of "self-talk," the monologue that goes on inside your head. Sometimes, conversations with yourself can reveal ways that you block your progress; other quiet contemplations can disclose great ideas and solutions to challenges. You can be your own best coach by asking yourself essential, powerful questions. Try these at least once per month.

What relationships do I need to deepen? Review your WHOs List. Think about HOWs that will keep key relationships moving forward. Here are some important, related questions:

> Who are important connectors and ideal clients you have only begun to get to know?

> When was the last time you updated information about your key contacts across all FORD areas?

> What relationships need to be refreshed because you haven't spoken to the person in awhile?

> Think about people you consider your "top priorities." What legal issues might be impacting them?

Keep in mind that developing business requires that you be proactive with your discussions, that you stay on people's radar screens and that they constantly expand their awareness of you as a person they trust, enjoy working with and in whom they are confident.

What personal and professional activities will be occupying your time in the next thirty days? How can you prepare for them? In order to support your commitment to create a solid return on investment (especially of your time!) throughout all of your activities, you must ask yourself these two questions. Review your calendar closely; think about all personal activities (including children's soccer games, yoga classes, happy hours, lunch breaks) and how you might *choose* to initiate and expand relationships during these times. Note I used the word "choose." I did this to emphasize that you don't ALWAYS have to engage in business development—it *is* a choice, one that I encourage you to make consciously. Suppose you find yourself saying, "I really don't want to 'work' while I am at lunch" or at whatever activity you are thinking about. Follow this statement with, "Is there any kind of connecting activity that I *would* be comfortable doing?" For example, just saying, "How's work going?" (and listening to the answer) counts. You don't always have to roll out your Twenty Questions. If you are an introvert (or a tired extrovert), even saying "hello" in a friendly way counts. And, you can certainly take time off, bring a salad back to your office, close the door and read *People* magazine. Asking yourself to make a choice about how to engage in what is going on around you raises the likelihood that if you are going to "think business," you will do the preparatory thinking needed to be effective.

What do I need to be doing to connect for the first time with an ideal client? When you review your WHOs List, you find that you haven't come up with HOWs for a few of the newer entries. Here are some suggestions about ways to approach this task:

First, check to see if this client has ever been a client of the firm. Who was the relationship partner? Who worked on the matter? How long ago did the firm provide services to the individual or company? Are the people who worked with this person/company still at the firm? What was the matter? Was the work conducted out of your office or another office (if you are at a firm with multiple offices)? Make a note to speak with anyone in the firm who has been connected to this new individual/entity so that you can gather information that will help you devise an opening.

Second, does your firm have a contact relationship management system (CRM)? In case you are unfamiliar with CRMs, let me explain. This is a system where (theoretically) people enter names of people whom they have become familiar with so that other people in the firm can use their in-firm colleagues as connectors. Unfortunately, the more competitive a comp system is, the less attorneys seem to use this, preferring to keep relationships to themselves. However, it is definitely worth checking your CRM system or asking your business development professionals if such a system exists so you can determine a potential path to meeting or obtaining information about a new individual.

Remember to think about needs. If the person you are thinking about is an ideal client, what do you know about him/her? If your knowledge is minimal, use a search engine. Refer to the charts on pages 76 and 77 to review important information to gather about new (and existing) WHOs. As you record data, think about *potential* legal needs. If they are a member of the industry niche you are focusing on, make notes about what legal needs you have learned exist in similar companies. At some point you will want to know if this company has those needs too. What other opportunities might exist? Are they expanding? Do they have new products? Is their workforce downsizing or increasing? Do they have an IPO? Are they acquiring smaller companies or selling parts of their own? Think expansively. The information that you collect will provide directions about ways to approach this ideal client.

Next, plug this company or individual in to LinkedIn. Do you have connections in common? How might you want to leverage these connections? Fight all urges to think, "Connecting isn't possible," and "I could never reach out to that person or company." Consider all ideas; make choices about what action(s) seems best and/or most comfortable and authentic later.

Remember you do not have to take all of the actions at once. Budget your business development time. For example, if you can focus on business development for five minutes per day, divide a given task into five-minute allotments or set a timer for five minutes and do what you can until the bell rings.

How can I be a source of continual value to those in my network? We talked about this earlier: knowledge and connections are the king/queen of value. Are you up to speed on these commodities? What are you doing to consistently scan the enormous universe of information to gather trends and maintain awareness of the comings and goings that are important to your various WHOs? Do you have mechanisms to float information TO you? Do you have a formal or informal team of colleagues who are gathering and sharing information with each other? Are you pushing the information out to relevant WHOs? How about connections—are you introducing people to each other? Have you become a convener, bringing people together for lunch, happy hours, dinner, sports events, etc.? Let's say your answer to all of these questions is "yes." I'm not going to let you off the hook with that answer, although, first, let me congratulate you for being diligent and smart! Now let me ask you this: What do you need to do to take each one of these actions up one notch?

This is a particularly important question to ask yourself when and if you are feeling down about business being slow (this happens to everyone!). Keep the formula in mind about the power of sustaining relationships. Getting in front of people in a way that is relevant to them not only keeps relationships fresh, but underscores your focus on *their* needs, not just *your* need to get their business. It also *concretely shows* what most law firms state on their websites and say in their pitches about how they keep the clients' needs in mind. Go beyond client alerts in what you provide, although client alerts can be very helpful to your WHOs. Keep letting them know that you pay attention to their current events, to changes in their business and industry and that you, proactively, have ideas and connections that can help. It's okay if the ideas that you share are outside of the legal realm; for example, if you are working with an investment group, you might have an idea for a product that one of their companies could add to their product line, or you might have an idea for marketing. It doesn't matter whether your idea is brilliant or not. What matters is that you display, through your actions, that you consider yourself to be a part of their team—even if you have never done work for them. What better person to use as a lawyer than one who gives them something for free?

How can I leverage my activities? The word "leverage" is the professional word for what I casually call "double dipping," or "doing two things at once." If you are someone who feels very pressured by many personal and professional demands on your time, you must become a "professional double dipper." Here's how you do it: Review every one of your activities, personal and professional, and ask yourself if there is any way you can easily add a business development conversation. Don't think asking for business; instead think about ways to insert engaging in casual, friendly, interesting business *chat* into the activity. Going to a wedding? Set a goal to discover where three people work and learn about the most exciting parts of their jobs. How does this help you with business? (You should know the answer by now, but just to remind you—it allows you to find out if they are a connector or a potential client you should follow up with later.) Planning to watch your favorite television show? Pick up a business magazine to scan during the commercials. Helping your children with homework? Model Mom or Dad also doing "homework" by writing in your journal, sending notes to clients, etc. If you are a real extrovert and going to the bank, consider meeting with the bank manager to see if there are other customers of the bank that he/she could introduce to you. They really like doing this, as it is a value add for their customers.

The concept of inserting business into all that you are doing may feel burdensome at first, but this is because you haven't done it before. The more you do it, the more it will become automatic, something that you naturally blend into the way you go about your daily activities. Similarly, if the idea feels unnatural and not authentic, even pushy,

I recommend that you experiment and discover YOUR Way of asking people about how they spend time during the day in ways that are respectful, curious and convey the thought, "I really want to know about you." And, of course, if you don't want to do this, it's okay. There are many ways to develop valuable relationships. YOUR Way is the most important way.

Chapter 27

Goals—Make Them, Review Them, Commit to Them

Goals are one of the most important cornerstones of success. Short-term, intermediate and long-term goals keep us directed and focused. They help us measure how we are doing. There is a lot of science and guidance out there about the ways to set goals. Here's the bottom line: state them so you can answer the questions: "Did I do it?" and "Did I cross that mile marker?"

Taking action, checking a goal off your to-do list, regardless of the size, is an antidote for feeling discouraged and overwhelmed, and can also be a source of excitement, as completing a goal is a reason to celebrate.

Let's start with *immediate, short-term goals*. They are countable, detailed and small. There is no wiggle room in the interpretation of whether you did it or not. Given your time pressures, sometimes you may want to state an immediate goal in terms of time: "I am going to spend five minutes listing technology companies in my city that I find from a Google search," or "I am going to spend ten minutes writing down highlights of an article that I want to send to some of my WHOs." Some consultants may not approve of stating goals in time terms, as accomplishments can be relatively vague—you worked for five minutes but in reality stared at page four the entire time. However, sometimes, setting five minutes aside for business development and using that time in whatever way you can is often all you can do. So I prefer that you be kind to yourself and define goals in terms of time if it fits your style and propels you to take *some kind* of action.

The other method of setting immediate goals is listing specific, observable tasks such as making two phone calls, stopping by a specific partner's office, sending an e-mail to three people on your WHOs List, etc. Otherwise called a to-do list.

I once asked a very successful rainmaker what he believed was the one tool that had the highest impact on his huge book of business. He replied, "Every Monday morning at

8:00 a.m. I make a list of thirty business development activities I am going to accomplish that week. I get those things done **no matter what.** If I manage to check everything off the list by Wednesday, I add twenty more things." His emphasis on the phrase "no matter what" really caught my attention, as I imagine it did yours, so I asked him to elaborate: "How do you get your whole list done with all you have on your plate?" He responded in a very cut and dry tone that underscored his commitment, "I just do. There are no other choices. I just get them done."

I strongly encourage you to keep your immediate goals very small, so that they are accomplishable. When you set your immediate goals, articulate them *and* write them down as singular activities. The goal "Get to know practice group leader (Alice)" is too general and will take months, maybe longer, to achieve. In the immediate term, this general goal is comprised of a set of immediate, minute actions such as:

> Stop by Alice's office on Monday, have casual conversation, such as about weekend
>
> Provide article about CEO of XYZ Tech (her client)
>
> Obtain list of Alice's current clients from business development manager
>
> Spend five minutes a day constructing a list of ways I can add value to each of her clients
>
> Offer to introduce Alice to Tim, GC of ABC Tech

Notice the specificity of the above list. When you are specific, you can determine exactly what to do and know when it is done.

Here is a creative tip: write your weekly business development goals on neon-colored paper, preferably the same color each time. This activity accomplishes two things: 1) it will not get lost on your desk among all the other papers; and 2) over time, you will associate the color with business development actions; seeing the color will attract your attention and become an integral part of your ongoing thinking process.

ACTION: Make a list of goals to accomplish this week.

I state my ***intermediate goals*** in general, directional terms to express where I want to end up within a relatively brief period of time, such as six months. For example: I want to research the top twenty companies on my WHOs List or I want to pull together a group of ten women CEOs. Experiment with different time intervals for *intermediate goals*, such as monthly or quarterly, to see what interval(s) best facilitates your momentum and planning. Decide the best place to record your goals: your business development journal/diary, a periodic "goal sheet" or another option. As a reminder, writing your goals is important. The action of deliberately recording a goal, whether via keyboard or pen, is akin to making a commitment. And, there is some science that indicates that the recording process activates a section of the brain that supports the goal acquisition process. (See Henriette Anne Klauser, *Write It Down, Make It Happen*.)

ACTION: Make a list of goals to be accomplished in the next six months.

The importance of having **long-term goals** (sometimes called Career Purpose) and a vision of success cannot be stated too often. We discussed BHAGs (Big Hairy Audacious Goals) earlier in the book. I celebrate Jim Collins's differentiation between a bad BHAG and a good BHAG: *"Bad BHAGS, it turns out, are set with bravado; good BHAGs are set with understanding"* (*Good to Great*). Taking the time to understand what is truly important to you so that you can work toward it is a motivating, inspirational and uplifting reminder on those days you question the purpose of some of the drudgery that accompanies ALL careers. If, over a period of time, say three months, you cannot detect or identify an alignment between your daily activities and your long-term goals (what you are doing is not, in any way, moving you toward what you value), then stop, reflect and ask yourself tough questions such as: what can I do to alter my activities so that they better match what I ultimately want in my career; to what degree do my daily activities help me build the skills and knowledge I need to acquire my long-term goals; what changes within my current job do I need to make; do I need to look for another workplace to pursue my goals; would speaking with someone (person to be determined) to help me develop the insight I need to make needed adjustments be helpful?

ACTION: Review professional, long-term goals to make sure that they reflect *your* definition of a gratifying professional life.

Finally, if your business development direction feels ineffective, random and/or unclear, review, fine-tune and recommit to new short-term, immediate-term and long-term goals.

Tips to Taking Smart Action

1. *Have a plan—keep it visible.* People who can easily see their plan are more likely to act on it. I like to use bulletin boards. Try not to fall prey to the "out of sight, out of mind" trap by putting your plan in a computer file that you never see or

in a journal that you never open. Your business development goals and plan are instrumental to professional success. Put it where it can "smile" at you throughout the day. Many lawyers don't want to place their plan where others can see it. Here are some other ideas about where to put it: inside your top desk drawer; in a closed, neon-colored folder on your desk; on the inside door of a cabinet you use often.

ACTION: Decide where to "post" your plan and your short-term goal list.

2. *Create changing, multiple tiers in your WHOs List.* Most people have a love/hate relationship with their WHOs List; on the one hand they find it to be a great way to capture and track people and companies to help them make rain; on the other hand, the list feels long, unwieldy and overwhelming, Creating tiers, monthly focuses, priority categories or any kind of divisions that make sense to you will help. There are many ways to slice and dice the WHOs List so that you can take sensible action. Earlier, we discussed creating repeatable schedules, with electronic reminders, to make sure you sustain contact with people. That system will organize your WHOs a great deal. Another way to approach taking action with your WHOs List is to periodically create categories of WHOs to whom you want to pay *special* attention. The categories could correspond to your perception of a need that they might have, their connection to a hot topic that is of immediate interest or even your belief that you will see the individuals at an upcoming meeting. When I travel, I refer to my WHOs List to see who is located in the city I plan to visit. These people I elevate to high priority status. Sometimes people or companies have designated periods when they open their legal panels for new participants or engage in some kind of planning process in which you want to be sure you are included. This would also elevate the company to a high priority status. A final idea about WHOs to prioritize: stay in touch with former clients—it is easier to get a second matter with someone who already knows you than a first one with someone for whom you have not yet worked.

ACTION: List ten high-priority WHOs to focus on during the next month; schedule time to research and prepare your conversations.

3. *Create daily, weekly, monthly and quarterly goals.* Think of your goals as your weekend errands list: where do you need to go, what do you need to do, what route are you taking to get there? Check the task off the list when it is done.

ACTION: Decide what you will accomplish today, by next Friday, by the end of this month, by the end of this quarter.

4. *Specifically defined immediate goals create traction; broadly articulated immediate goals block momentum, as the actions needed to move ahead are not clear.* When (not if, as we all get there from time to time) you feel stuck and unmotivated, ask yourself, "What is one clear action I can say 'yes' to doing?" If you are tired, it might just be researching something on the web or organizing your WHOs List. Success happens one specific action at a time. Choose one small task and get it done.

   ACTION: What can you say "yes" to doing before you go to sleep tonight?

5. *Rigorously use your calendar to plan business development activities.* Among the biggest struggles I see would-be rainmakers have is figuring out how to balance attention to ongoing client work with attention to developing potential client work. Your calendar can help by scheduling time for yourself just as you would for a client. One attorney with whom I worked chose a name for her business development time: Roy Smith. When Roy Smith appeared in her schedule, she closed the door and "met" with him. For this lawyer, giving business development a name placed it on the same plane of importance as client work. However you choose to make business development a priority, relegating specific time for it on your calendar will help it feel legitimate and important, which it is, even though not billable. When you cancel on yourself, you are saying that you and your success are not important. Is this how you feel? Of course not. What would you do if you sprained your ankle and HAD to go to the emergency room? You would figure out a way to attend to your needs and somehow all would turn out okay. Think of your ankle. Don't cancel your appointment with you most important client—you.

   ACTION: Schedule a time this week to think about business development.

   Thinking need not be a passive, vague activity, especially when it comes to business development. I find it important to take time and review the effectiveness of my activities, consider new ways to move forward and brainstorm means to connect with important people. Often, in my zeal to achieve, I move so quickly that I lose the creativity that comes from quiet reflection: a fine-tuned strategy, realigned plans and lessons learned from failures and successes.

Chapter 28

Do I Want or Need a Coach?

W hat resources, outside yourself, do you need to take action toward developing business, *no matter what?* Who would be your muse? What would be your motivator(s)? Who can give you the kind push you need to inspire you, give you ideas when you're stuck, help you figure out your blocks to moving forward and, with you, celebrate achievements? If your answer is "a personal trainer," "someone I don't know," "a professional who understands the ups and downs of getting ahead," then a coach is likely the one for you.

Coaches have become invaluable resources for many lawyers, and as is the case with all the tools and techniques described in this book, whether or not a coach will be helpful to you depends on how you learn and what resources have helped you grow and change throughout your life.

A coach helps individuals personalize and utilize generic, well-founded knowledge to successfully attain goals and behaviors. While coaches have different approaches and styles, most assist in areas such as:

- Identifying personal/professional values and goals
- Clarifying factors that impact motivation
- Developing a strategy and plan built upon personal components including strengths, approach to work/life, comfort zones, personal/professional resources and network, long-term goals
- Executing the plan
- Reflecting on each step of implementation so that constant learning and forward movement occurs
- Fine-tuning the plan
- Evaluating progress

- Supporting and encouraging
- Challenging "I can'ts"

Prior to engaging a coach, it is best to first learn about aspects that surround and comprise the target thought/skill set, in this case, business development. This can be accomplished through reading a book such as this one or attending a comprehensive workshop that addresses topics such as:

- The anatomy of the legal marketplace
- Ways to think about the importance of engaging in business
- Strategies for success
- Skills needed to attain and pursue success
- Approaches to leverage your style, way of thinking, comfort zone, etc.
- Metrics to assess growth
- Activities to increase motivation and momentum
- Resources that contribute to business development

After obtaining general knowledge about the context and skills of the behavior or goal that you want to acquire, coaching focuses on integrating and utilizing the knowledge YOUR Way, so success can be achieved.

The length of a successful individual coaching engagement is influenced by the styles of both individual and coach. Highly independent individuals might choose to finish coaching when a plan has been created and pursue implementation on their own, while an individual who likes "talking things over" might find longer-term conversations with a coach clarifying and motivational. Despite the length of a coaching program, continuing the gains made during coaching when the meetings have concluded presents a profound challenge to achieving a substantial return on investment. Before finishing your engagement with a coach, be very clear about how you are going to sustain the momentum made during coaching. You might even want to phase out coaching slowly so that you are sure that you have successfully transitioned from having a "silent partner-guide-cheerleader" to working on your own.

While there are people who seem to be "born rainmakers," most of us must learn, fail, struggle and celebrate small steps along the way. During your first phase of coaching I recommend exploring your strengths, goals and WHATs, and then move toward putting them into a strategy that fits for you. Finish your first stage with a WHOs List and a Blueprint.

In Phase 2, the coach can help you execute your strategy. The beginning of implementation can be difficult, as momentum can occur slowly. It is important during the early part of this phase to not focus on obtaining business, but gradually identify and create sustained relationships and put systems in place. Having a coach in your corner to encourage you, process the difficulties and figure out how to take advantage of opportunities can be instrumental.

The coaching industry has become large and diverse with respect to coaching philosophies, tools and techniques. For the purposes of developing business, I am biased toward a coaching methodology that includes direct guidance about business development strategies, techniques and tools, and helps an individual investigate topics related to his/her motivation, coping with challenges, values and ways to comfortably integrate business development activities into his/her life. I am less inclined to embrace a coaching philosophy that is weighted toward exploration and personal discovery. I also strongly believe in utilizing a coach who has worked extensively in the legal industry and is knowledgeable about the legal marketplace and importance of business development for attorneys. Coaches come in many shapes and sizes: some are former lawyers, some have worked extensively in corporate settings, and many have backgrounds in human resources, psychology, counseling, etc. Yet those most prepared to provide significant benefit for lawyers possess coach training, and extensive experience working as a coach, have spent time under the tutelage of a seasoned coach and have researched and understand the legal marketplace.

Interview coaches to find a coach whose style seems the best fit for the way you learn; one who possesses the background that you believe provides the best preparation to offer insights you deem important, and also has other characteristics such as gender, ethnicity, age, etc., that will allow you to forge the strongest possible working relationship.

Finding a coach who can help you with business development is easy today with Internet technology. Certainly, Google and LinkedIn are excellent search engines, although they do not vet your findings. Here are a few other resources:

Threshold Advisors—www.ThresholdAdvisors.com: Full disclosure—this is my firm's website. My partners and affiliating coaches are very experienced strategic business development coaches, AND we are all happy to provide the names of other fabulous coaching colleagues.

Your firm: a growing number of firms have vetted coaches for a variety of assignments. Ask professionals focused on professional development, business development and diversity for coaches who have had successful experiences with the firm.

Organizations focused on the legal industry: ABA, Legal Marketing Association, National Association of Law Placement, Association of Law Firm Diversity Professionals, National Association of Women Lawyers, among others—these organizations have spotlighted coaching at their various conferences. Look at conference agendas to find names of speakers on various topics related to coaching, business development and career advancement.

A final note about individual coaching: Many of us who coach lawyers experience the frustrating phenomenon of last-minute appointment cancellations. Reasons range from personal circumstances to "last-minute client emergencies." While these occurrences are inconvenient to us, I am more concerned about what they *may* represent in many cases: that business development activities take a back seat to other concerns. I see my time coaching clients about business development as a temporary placeholder for the time that the individual will use to focus on rainmaking when he/she is no longer using a coach. This note may not be applicable to you. If it does strike a chord, even a quiet sound of familiarity, think about how you prioritize business development, remind yourself of the impact that increased business will have on your personal and professional life and work toward creating ways to maintain its significance in your daily activities.

Having an individual coach is not the only way to get your process started and solidly moving ahead. Of course, you can use this book as a guide and can work on your own, step-by-step. Also, consider having a "buddy coach," a colleague or friend with whom you can discuss goals, grapple with questions and discuss strategies. A buddy coach is especially valuable after you have a strategy in hand. I know a pair of attorneys who get together for breakfast every Friday morning at 8:00 a.m. They talk about the actions they took during the week, progress they are making toward closing business, hesitations and ideas. They are wonderful advocates for each other and challenge each other when progress stalls. Surprising to both of them, they have found ways to reach out to ideal clients together. They have become true partners.

Collaborating with a small group of like-minded colleagues can produce many benefits in addition to supporting each other to make rain. Think of the group as a firm within a firm where, as a group, you have a vision of success, strategic objectives and a plan that involves integrating the relationships, skills, strengths and differences of all involved. I recognize that firm compensation structures can add a note of confusion (to say the least) when figuring out the specific financial benefits of working as a team. In order to keep this elephant from crushing the richness that a collaborative approach can yield, I suggest adopting an outlook that emphasizes the notion that when people help each other and leverage their relationships and knowledge, everyone will thrive in some way, shape or form.

Teamwork that produces rain can operate in many, different ways. The least formal group can meet periodically, such as once per month, and adopt a show-and-tell format where participants share progress, ask for specific introductions and exchange ideas. The other side of the spectrum utilizes a more cohesive team format where the team strategizes and executes as a unit, for example, they choose an industry niche to penetrate across the practice groups of all attorneys in the group.

Whatever the central purpose of a collaborating group, I recommend that the following components are utilized to some extent:

- Everyone must be committed to rigorously helping each other succeed and be willing to ask and give.

- Exchange details about each other's practices, relationships, industry focus, goals, people/companies each would like to know and know better. At first this may seem to be a cumbersome activity; if so, break it into different segments, for example: discuss industry focus at one meeting, target relationships at another, etc. The more information you have about each other, the more you can assist each other and know how to leverage the attributes and relationships that each person brings to the table, the more successful the group will be.

- Be clear about the purpose of the collaboration and what each member is expected to contribute.

- Emphasize the importance of meeting attendance and active participation; valuable collaboration is built upon these elements. If people stop coming, ask what the group can do differently to elevate the value of the group so that most people will come most of the time.

- Expect conflict and differences of opinion. Create mechanisms to work through disagreements so that trust builds after clashes.

- Schedule time for the group to evaluate its strengths and weaknesses to make sure that it continuously grows stronger, more vibrant and valuable.

- Consider utilizing an outside group facilitator from time to time to help the group delve into subjects that it might either be avoiding or not know to discuss.

- Attend to the level of participation of each group member to make sure that no one dominates discussions, is not contributing or remains on the periphery of conversations. Of course, people behave differently in groups; however, strong groups possess a norm of some degree of participation from all members.

- Communicating between meetings keeps group members connected, thinking about ways to help each other, and keeps conversations flourishing.

I am an *extremely* strong believer in the power of business development collaboration. If I was a managing partner, practice group leader or any level of lawyer in a firm, I would get together with others to cultivate success and create any structures needed, such as compensation structures, to promote this modality. If you are standing up saying, "YES, LET'S DO IT!" I am thrilled. In a profession such as the law, with a strong tradition of individuality, many if not most lawyers lack the skills and strategies needed to be strong business development collaborators and leaders of business development collaborative teams. Learning these skills through workshops, reading (*All for One* by Andrew Sobel) and/or coaching will reap a solid return on your investment.

Chapter 29

What Do I Do When There Doesn't Seem to Be Any Work?

There is no business I know of, and remember you are in the *business* of law, that isn't confronted with this painful question from time to time. As I write this, many law firms are asking themselves this about litigation. In 2008 M&A lawyers were baffled by this reality. Slow business times are scary. Don't let these periods paralyze you; take action.

First, in the relationship realm, spend significant time with your WHOs List. Remember the more active, fresh, meaningful relationships you have, the higher your likelihood of business. Here are some things to consider:

1. What relationships need refreshing?

2. Add people to your WHOs List and make a plan to initiate and/or expand your relationships with them.

3. Get in touch with clients and all individuals with whom you have worked in the recent past and see how they are doing since your work together.

4. Spend time on LinkedIn to see where your relationships may be today.

5. What is currently important to your WHOs?

6. Talk to connectors. See what insights they might have for directions and people to reach out to.

7. Attend networking events with the goal of exploring changes in the marketplace. Ask direct questions about legal issues that impact your area of expertise to determine directions that you might go.

Next, in the spirit of the movie *All the President's Men,* you must "follow the money." Among the wonderful aspects of being a lawyer is that all businesses need lawyers. Your challenge is to keep finding ways to position and reposition yourself so that you have value or so that you can bring in business for colleagues who can provide services for which you can obtain credit. You are not alone in having to be flexible with how you define your professional skills over the course of your career—most professionals and businesses expect it sometime during the tenure of their vocation. Here are questions to help you assess the marketplace so that you can consider repositioning:

1. What areas of the law **are** active right now? Is this a trend or a shift that is likely to be around for a while? How can I be a part of this development? Do I need to develop new knowledge? Is there a way to *slightly* alter what I do to participate in the prosperous areas?

2. What **firms** are active in my area? What are they doing to be involved in the marketplace?

3. Which **lawyers** in my firm are busy? How can I add value to them?

4. Are there any **industries** that are actively using lawyers more than others? If so, start the relationship development process there.

Now look at hot and/or up-and-coming trends in your practice area and across industries.

1. What legal issues are people discussing and thinking are on the threshold of concern or opportunity?

2. What industries might be impacted by changes in the law, new decisions, product lines, current events, etc? How can you position yourself to move with these changes?

3. Might learning anything new make you more attractive and valuable to potential clients in the near future?

I do a lot of self-reflecting during the slow times to make sure that I am coming across in ways that I want to be seen. Perhaps I have inadvertently been focusing on my needs as opposed to others. Maybe I have not been giving and offering. I evaluate if I am rigorously following my game plan, and make sure that I am thinking as expansively as I need to in order to achieve my long-term goals. Often these questions are not easy, yet they are essential to shed light on ways to move forward:

1. How is my firm doing in general? Is my slow time tied to difficulties in the firm?

2. Might my slow time be indicative of changes in the firm? What do I have to do to be strongly positioned if changes are to occur such as a change in leadership?

3. Am I aligned with the firm's current business development priorities and directions? If not, is this still the right firm for me? You don't need to do anything dramatic if you are questioning. Quietly ask colleagues in other firms about their experiences and gather information that helps you decide whether more decisive action is needed.

4. How extensively do people know about me, my skills and the depth of my expertise? Do I need to be more active on social media and/or traditional media? Do I need to do more speaking, writing, etc.?

5. How am I viewed inside the firm? Ask your practice group leaders, colleagues with more and less experience than you, the office/firm managing partner, your assistant, etc., for feedback. Have you acquired leadership positions that will help you expand your connections in the firm and be seen as a valuable colleague? Are you contributing on firm committees or even contributing so much that that you do not have time to attend to business development?

6. Where else might I fit in within the legal community? Are there in-house opportunities? Teaching opportunities? Other places to flex your legal muscles?

7. Do I want to keep practicing law?

These are a lot of questions and I am sure you can think of more. Please remember that slow time and career changes are absolutely normal in lifelong careers. I find it funny—it's during the hard, scary times that I become the most creative in my professional pursuits and give myself permission to attempt directions that I wouldn't do when I am busy. One person I know called it "the creativity and gift of desperation." So, while these career times have frightening elements, I also know them to be important, clarifying times. Hang in there, ask the hard questions and take action.

Part VI

The Psychology of Making Rain

One of my value propositions to the legal industry is that I am one of the few psychologists who specializes in work with lawyers and organizations in which they work. Since growth, behavior change and maintenance, personality, relationships, emotions and people in general are a part of my professional background, I wanted to connect concepts that are basic to me as a psychologist with the development of rainmakers.

Our life is comprised of continuously evolving behaviors. As we get older, we choose to develop certain behaviors such as learning to knit, learning a new language and learning to become an elite athlete of some sort. Most behaviors we acquire gradually, although some of us push to learn along a rapid learning curve. Foundational to all growth are psychological characteristics, some impacted significantly by our unique biological make-up, others influenced predominantly by our family, background and experience. These features affect the ways we respond and use new skills and ideas. I am frequently asked if rainmaking can be taught. My quick response is "Largely yes." The more extensive response is "Yes. Some individuals are natural rainmakers and need relatively no education. Nature AND nurture provided them with the perfect mixture of ingredients. The rest of us can definitely learn to be business developers." However, our success will be significantly impacted by the way we handle some basic psychological constructs, several of which I will briefly explain below.

Chapter 30

Pessimism

Martin Seligman, a psychologist and founder of the positive psychology movement, defines pessimism as the belief that troubles last forever, undermine everything and are uncontrollable. He emphasizes that it is less about a "glass half empty" attitude than a pervasive focus on problems and why things won't work. In the book *Authentic Happiness: Using the New Positive Psychology to Realize Your Potential for Lasting Fulfillment,* Seligman notes that among the wide field of professionals, attorneys have among the highest levels of pessimism. However, he is perceptive to point out that this outlook serves them in their substantive endeavors, as it "enables a good lawyer to see every conceivable snare and catastrophe that might occur in any transaction. The ability to anticipate the whole range of problems and betrayals that nonlawyers are blind to is highly adaptive for the practicing lawyer who can, by so doing, help his clients defend against these far-fetched eventualities." I am starting this section with pessimism as, while it may help you help clients, a positive focus is essential in rainmaking. Thinking positively supports you to pursue new possibilities and relationships and enables you to try the multitude of approaches that are necessary to find YOUR Way.

With a smile on my face, my mind immediately turns to a forty-year-old male partner at a small law firm who came to me for help. The first words out of his mouth were, "I really want to develop a book of business but I can't see it happening. After all, I am a lawyer and we are all pessimists." And then he laughed. You have to have a sense of humor about yourself to go anywhere in life. I particularly appreciated his level of self-awareness in this area and encourage you to listen to your own thinking as you develop and implement business development strategies. The words "yes, but" are the flashing red lights of pessimism. For example, whenever I gave the above lawyer, Larry, an idea, he would spend the next fifteen minutes telling me why it wouldn't work. While our back and forth about what would and wouldn't work could be exhausting, what I learned from Larry is that there were usually important elements in his pessimistic viewpoints that behooved us to take into consideration as we strategized. It was essential that we never dismissed a negative "push back" outright. For example, when we discussed an industry focus, he thoroughly argued that none were appropriate to his practice, even though he conceded that if he pursued business one industry at a time, his rainmaking activities would be efficient. We spoke extensively about his viewpoint and discovered that he was *afraid* that the locale in which he wanted to work would not support him working only in one industry niche. "*AH,*" I said, "Let's research this and see. Perhaps you will need to pursue a few niches. Can we begin with one and see what happens?" Once he knew that his viewpoints were taken into consideration, and even made some sense to me, we were able to move ahead. Originally, Larry wanted to dismiss the concept of industry niche totally. As we explored and integrated parts of his concerns into the strategy, we were able to move forward without the pessimism and with a smart plan.

Here's what Larry's experience has to offer you: recognize that you have tendencies to evaluate activities in terms of won't work. Listen for the voice inside of you that presents so many roadblocks that you are not able to take *any* business action. Commit to not stopping at this wall. Ask *what parts* of the pessimistic viewpoint *can* be used to create an approach that you *are* willing to take. And, finally, when you come up with what I call "an acceptable idea," do it; do not tolerate inaction. However, you internally calculate the likelihood of success. A great function for a coach is to balance your pessimism with positive perspectives. Because Larry trusted my approach and experiences, he was willing to move forward even when he had doubts. Larry allowed me to push him when I thought he was being too pessimistic and I made sure that I never discarded his opinions outright. Rather, I did my best to help him use his cautiousness to craft positive action.

Avoid what won't work and challenge yourself to find something that *may*.

Our next topic, perfectionism, often works alongside pessimism to halt or slow business development momentum.

✎

Chapter 31

Perfectionism

Perfectionism is the pursuit of something impossible: a body, a work product, a relationship, etc., with no flaws. Perhaps machines are capable of creating such an entity, but humans, largely, are not. Yet there is a voice within many of us, again, particularly lawyers and, interestingly, particularly women lawyers, that says, "More, better ... more, better." The result of such a cycle is often that too much time is spent on something with relatively little gain. For example, you may stay up all night putting together an opinion for a client who would have been thrilled by the 11:00 p.m. version. Perfectionism shows up in rainmaking when lawyers critique themselves to be "not good enough ... yet"; not smart enough, capable enough, experienced enough, old enough, ready enough to let people know that they can do and/or lead efforts to attend to their legal needs. As a result, you stay in roles of "serving" others instead of pursuing your own goals. Not only does perfectionism keep you from thriving in what is important to you, but when you elect to only work on others' matters, you are vulnerable to downturns in the economy or any other changes that could result in your talents not being needed. Having a book of business gives you the greatest ability to bob and weave with changes in the industry.

All of what we have discussed in this book can be hindered and/or halted by your need to be perfect. For example, many lawyers stay stuck thinking about a perfect strategy because they can't select a "perfect" niche. In that case, we review criteria that comprise a "strong niche" and compare their niche ideas to the list. Yet, despite their niche ideas complying with the standards, they continue to be plagued by "I don't know, it still doesn't feel right." Other attorneys are haunted by fears that a given event isn't the "perfect" one to attend. I help them think through their concerns and ask if there is a high likelihood that some WHOs will be in the room. "Yes," they tell me after having completed research. And then, you know what they (maybe you?) say? "I don't know, it just doesn't feel like the right event to go to." I can provide many examples.

From what many of you and my lawyer colleagues have shared with me, most of you come by the perfectionism trait quite honestly, after having been an associate to very tough partners who red-lined your work to such an extent that you learned that there is no such thing as an acceptable work product. I'll call this phenomenon a form of Post-Traumatic Stress Disorder (PTSD), where individuals are plagued by horrendous past events.

At its most constructive, striving toward perfectionism can be thought of as a *pursuit* of excellence, not a requirement that the end product be excellent AND totally flawless. This doable frame of mind allows you to stretch to achieve and learn without an expectation of a finale that is truly unattainable.

As a growing rainmaker (and all of you are), I want to encourage you to embrace imperfection! Every time you step out of your comfort zone to meet a new person, attempt a conversation in a new way, send an e-mail to someone who seems unlikely to return your note, hear me congratulate you. These efforts tell me and you that your rainmaking muscles are being exercised and thereby getting stronger every day.

At a recent Ms. JD Conference I had the pleasure of hearing Reshma Saujani, author of *Women Who Don't Wait in Line*, speak. She said that while she appreciates receiving positive feedback, what she treasures most is hearing about things that would make her presentation or work better received or stronger. People who honor her with such input earn her trust. "If you are honest about growing, ask for what you didn't do well," she said, while acknowledging that, at first, this is an emotionally difficult request to make.

To make perfectionism your friend, turn it from a descriptor of an action ("I did this perfectly!") to an ideal that motivates you ("I aim toward ...") Know when "excellence" is needed, such as in your client work, and when "good enough" will accomplish your goals, such as in the preparatory phase of going to an event. If you find yourself taking an extraordinarily long time to complete a task, ask yourself if your standards are getting in the way of completion. When hesitating to step outside of your comfort zone in fear that your actions will be subpar (in *your* evaluation), set basic and acceptable criteria for the action and, instead, reward the courage needed to stretch.

In psychology we have a concept called "framing," just as when you frame a picture in many different settings and achieve a slightly different look due to the edging. In psychology we use framing to describe how our feelings about a given event are changed by applying different attitudes. Framing a concept is the meaning we put to it—if we frame, or believe, we will be fired from our job if we act in a certain way, we will likely feel anxious as we work on the task. With this in mind, instead of framing rainmaking as an activity that can only be conducted by the most brilliant, competent, perfect attorneys, reframe it as an enjoyable opportunity to meet interesting people; engage in fun, valuable relationships; and offer valuable contributions to make a difference in someone's life. The first attitude will block your abilities to engage in business development; the second attitude makes it similar to the typical socializing that you do, and therefore, makes it doable. People engage lawyers they like, who they believe can comfortably navigate them through a cumbersome, often frightening legal maze. Such individuals are not perfect; they are human, trustworthy and caring. Strive to be human and you can make it rain.

Chapter 32

Fear of Failure

People ask me all the time if I like working with lawyers. Frankly, I find that a perplexing question; I mean, why wouldn't I like working with lawyers? All of that aside, I am very respectful of the long path that you have followed to get where you are today: good grades in high school, top of the class in college, surviving the rigors of law school (I can't imagine!) and the very steep learning curve that occupies your attention to provide each client what they need every day. My awe of you is huge! My admiration is coupled with concern for each of you as you face the rigors of constant evaluation from senior lawyers, clients and the firm. You have shared that fear of failing occupies many of your thoughts on an ongoing basis.

Creating new ways to look at actions that fall short of expectations (yours and others') is essential to grow and advance. The name of one of the chapters in Reshma Saujani's book *Women Who Don't Wait in Line* and wisdom within the section shares a fresh and critical outlook: "Fail Fast, Fail First, Fail Hard." In this chapter says, "If you haven't failed in your life, it means you haven't taken enough risks. Period. And if you haven't taken enough risks, you're not living up to your true potential ... As you aim to advance in your career, stop taking those professional baby steps and lay down some bold steppingstones instead. Take stretch assignments that will prepare you for the job you want." Take this to heart. Create a pathway of small steps that gives you experience managing the inner voice that fears the failure lest calamity occur. Here are some activities to try in the business development realm to help you experience the learning potential of trying new things. As you debrief each "effort," write down what went well and what you would like to do differently next time. There are no failures, only learning experiences:

1. Talk to someone inside the firm whom you do not know, who you deem is powerful and "beyond" you. Discuss something about which you feel comfortable or ask this person a simple question about his/her experiences.

2. Go to an event where you think there will be no one you know in attendance. Stay for ten minutes and speak to one person about why he/she chose to come to the event.

3. Make a list of dream clients, people/companies you would love to work with someday. When you hear a voice inside of you say, "That will never happen," respond by saying, "If it doesn't, it is okay. However, I am going to find ways to approach at least some of these people/companies."

4. Speak up at a meeting when you have an idea that is different from one someone already stated. Disregard any feedback you receive about whether the comment is "good" or "bad." You get a gold star for effort!

5. Ask a client for feedback about how well you are meeting his/her needs. Emphasize that you would like to know what you are doing that is meeting his/her needs and actions you could take that would increase his/her levels of satisfaction. Be proud that you asked; don't worry about the feedback.

6. Talk to a friend about his/her business. Don't ask for business. Aim to get a clear understanding of what his/her business does.

7. Ask someone you would like to be a client someday about the criteria that they use to choose outside counsel. Just gather information and be interested, don't talk about yourself or the firm.

8. Carve out thirty minutes of time to focus on business development, during which time you do not check your e-mail or answer a knock on your door. If you complete this, congratulate yourself for focusing only on *your* needs.

9. Ask a firm rainmaker if you can go with him/her to an event or a meeting where he/she is having a conversation with a potential client. If they say "no," push away any thoughts that lead you to wonder if they said "no" because they don't like you.

10. Spend five minutes imagining yourself as a prolific rainmaker who utilizes a style of connecting with people that feels authentic and natural to you.

Remember, most of us developed a fear of failure when we were very young. We experienced that in order to get love, approval and attention, we had to impress someone. Because of these experiences, it will likely take a long time and a lot of "experiments" to quiet your fears. Commit to increasing your awareness of when dread creeps in and, as such, you hesitate to act. In these moments ask yourself, "What **can** I say 'yes' to?"

and then see if you can challenge yourself to take one more degree of risk. Stretch forward toward your goals; it's worth a shot! Learn from failure—let failure be your best teacher.

Chapter 33

Resilience

Writing this book has been an interesting experience for me. Often, when I am feeling a bit stuck about how I want to say something, a person appears with a story that captures my point better than any professional discourse I could share. For example, I just hung up the phone with a woman partner I have known and worked with for a long time. She is a member of a litigation practice area where she is the only female. Recently, her longtime mentor and strong supporter resigned and moved away, curtailing her access to his guidance. Without his presence and sponsorship, opportunities seemed to dry up. Occasions where she would have gone into his office to strategize ways to navigate the "eat what you kill" culture left her without a sounding board and a bit lost. "I almost feel picked on now without Sam; I am not being given credit in situations where I deserve it. I don't know if I can stay here much longer, yet I don't know where to go." This is where possessing the skill and outlook of resilience comes into play: an ability and mindset that allows you to move through difficult situations and obstacles.

Researchers claim that much of resilience is learned. Think about your childhood; what did you learn about coping with adversity? How were you taught to think and act "when times get rough"? If you had experience in athletics, you no doubt learned ways to "suck it up," lose, and move on to the next game. Ways that your family dealt with difficult times, or, on the other hand, couldn't deal with life's complicated situations also provide models to handle complexities.

Lawyers must have strong resilience capabilities in order to "stay the course" and advance in the face of difficult clients, evolving models of practice, a plethora of back-to-back meetings, an ever-changing legal marketplace and their highly competitive work environments. Business development also presents challenges, not the least of which is finding time to do it! Other tough issues include the length of time it typically takes to develop a relationship that involves the engagement of legal services;

lack of responsiveness from people to whom you reach out; stepping outside your comfort zone to meet new people; not getting a piece of work you thought you were well-positioned to obtain; insecurity (do they like me, respect me, have confidence in my expertise?); etc.

A compilation of thinking from different psychologists and researchers yields a variety of strategies and techniques to put into your resilience tool box so that you can move forward when advancement feels impossible. Most translate into consistently using positive, forward-driving, self-affirming ways of thinking, approaching opportunities and conceptualizing adversity. Here are some examples of ways to think and actions to take:

1. Bear in mind that failure is an attitude. Reframe unsuccessful incidents by asking yourself: "What did this experience teach me? What can I do differently next time?"

2. In the "game of numbers," where you will try to meet people many ways and forge various connections, know that *everything* you try will not pan out as you hoped. Don't spend time being disappointed. Move on to the next possibility.

3. Create as large a WHOs List as you can to keep possibilities unlimited. With a large list in hand it is easy to ask yourself, "Who's next?" and feel resource-full as opposed to lost, scared and frustrated.

4. Remember the various teachings in this book: The stronger you build your relationships through giving and an awareness of the needs of others, the higher the likelihood that you will develop a positive, trusting brand that attracts people to you.

5. Do not let critical feedback discourage you. Just because someone perceives you in a certain way does not mean that this observation is accurate. Carefully consider feedback that you receive. You always have a choice about whether to use it or discard it. And, critical feedback does not make you "bad" (remember your tendency to be perfectionistic). Use input to help you grow, not beat you down.

6. Opportunities abound; the key is being a creative, out-of-the-box thinker. The irony of feeling desperate is that it often pushes you to be creative. Don't get down on yourself. Try something new and/or slightly uncomfortable.

7. There is nothing you "must" or "should" do (with appreciation to Dr. Albert Ellis). You have choices; choices have consequences, both positive and negative.

8. You are resource-full. When you feel stuck, ask for input and then make the decision that you deem is best for you at the time.

9. Life is a work in progress; the bumps will happen; keep moving ahead, "no matter what."

10. Supposedly, when trying to scale the mountain with elephants, Hannibal said, "I will find a way or make one." To that I add, "And nothing will deter me from reaching toward what is important to me."

Ideas such as the above form a resilient foundation. This is a strong psychological platform from which action and advancement can occur even in the face of the most frustrating circumstances.

Being a rainmaker requires that you consistently, courageously, drive ahead and that you take action, as the prolific rainmaker I quoted earlier in the book said, "No matter what." Business development can be difficult for many and is daunting for most. You can differentiate yourself from the pack by building "resiliency muscles." It's just like developing abdominal muscles; it requires time and a lot of exercise with heavy weights. Sometimes it may feel as though you are not making any progress, but don't despair, progress takes time. Be sure to stay aware of how your thinking is impacting your ability to sustain business development activity. When you feel frustrated, what are you saying to yourself? How can you change those thought patterns? When you are hesitant to talk with a potential client, check in with yourself about what internal messages are holding you back.

Developing business is doable. Be resilient, push through tough times, keep on going, no matter what ... it will happen.

Chapter 34

Confidence

The comprehensive research presented by Katty Kay and Claire Shipman in their 2014 book *The Confidence Code* brought the definition of and issues related to confidence front and center. Their definition of confidence is especially compelling: "The belief that you can create a successful outcome through action." Overall, succeeding builds confidence, particularly when a positive result comes from stepping outside your comfort zone or after learning from a previous failure. Both situations teach that positive outcomes can occur from re-approaching hurdles that had previously been experienced as insurmountable.

A discussion of confidence ties together most of what we have discussed in this section: in order to move rainmaking from daunting to doable, it is essential to confront internal beliefs that block your ability and willingness to move ahead. A frame of mind that purports "I can make it happen" fosters excitement and action flows. Here are suggestions and actions based on Kay and Shipman's observations applied to "The Psychology of Making Rain":

- Think positively about yourself and what you can make happen to drive action.

- Tolerate frustration, then turn to what you will try next.

- Learning to become a rainmaker is a gradual process. Sometimes you will judge your actions as effective; other times they will not accomplish your goals. This is the normal flow of growth. Learn to tolerate these ups and downs.

- The time between meeting people for the first time and having them become paying clients may be very long and, frequently, may not happen. Focusing on the fun and value of the relationship will keep the process positive. On the other hand, counting the days (years) in which a connection has not yielded business will make you feel discouraged and turn a given relationship negative.

- You can be seen in a positive and professional light no matter your age, gender, background, years of experience, etc. A giving nature, curiosity and warmth are valuable commodities that anyone can offer. When you lead with these aspects, you ARE a rainmaker.

- When in doubt, ask for encouragement and reminders that you CAN do it (we all need this from time to time, sometimes often!).

While some people seem to be born confident, optimistic and resilient, with no fear of failure and perfectionist tendencies in check, most of us are mere mortals and need to expand our current levels of these characteristics in order to achieve our definition of success. How do you do this? One step at a time. The process of growth starts with awareness—how confident, optimistic, etc., are you? There are some highly researched, validated assessments that can help you quantify your levels in the various areas.[4] Here is an alternative, more personal evaluative approach based on your vision of how you would like to portray each characteristic:

Take out a pad of paper. Write the characteristic you choose to focus on at the top of the page, such as "confidence," "courage in the face of failure," etc. Use one sheet of paper for each characteristic. Answer these two questions with respect to rainmaking as thoroughly as you can for each element:

1. Describe a highly (confident, resilient, courageous, optimistic) person. What behaviors does this person exhibit?

2. If you were as "x" (confident, resilient, courageous, optimistic) as you would ideally like to be, what are some things that you would do differently?

When you think of a highly confident rainmaker whom you know, or even imagine, what does he/she do on a daily basis to move his/her efforts forward? What does he/she do at trade event cocktail parties? Similar scenarios will help you in this exercise. Make sure that you list behaviors that you admire. For example, if you write down that when a confident rainmaker goes to a cocktail party he/she goes up to everyone, shakes their hand and talks constantly about how great he/she is, your image of a confident

---

4   One of the best resources for such assessments can be found at
     https://www.authentichappiness.sas.upenn.edu/testcenter.

rainmaker is likely negative and won't help you make a list of inspirational traits and behaviors. Take your time answering these questions over a few days.

With your lists of your ideals and things that you would do differently in hand, ask yourself one more question: What is one action that I am willing to take that will move me from how I see myself today toward behaviors and mindsets that I believe will allow me to be more successful? Remember: small, doable steps that will allow you to grow slowly and gradually will build your level of confidence.

Chapter 35

Identity

Little has been written about the impact of the way we see ourselves on rainmaking success, but it is important. Research has taught athletes that visualizing themselves performing successfully yields positive results; for example, divers see every twist and turn of their jump before doing it; golfers imagine a perfect swing (and even usually take a few practice swings before hitting); basketball players stand at the foul line, envisioning their arms reaching toward the hoop and releasing the ball at exactly the right time. You too must mentally practice acting like a rainmaker, internally talking about yourself in positive terms: "I am a successful rainmaker," "I am a growing rainmaker," "I am actively working on developing a huge book of business." When you use these kinds of phrases, both to yourself and/or to others, you psychologically are identifying with those qualities.

I am not at all suggesting that you use any phrases that are false, but that you adopt new ways of thinking about yourself. One day I called one of my clients, who had just reached her all-time largest book of business. I said, "Wow, you are a rainmaker!" She was silent for a moment—when you're coaching on the phone, "a moment" is a long time. "Am I a rainmaker?" she asked me. "Well, let's look at this objectively," I said. "You've brought in two significant clients over the past few months, haven't you? Isn't that what a rainmaker does?" "Oh, wow," she said, and then with glee, "I AM a rainmaker!"

Herminia Ibarra, Robin Ely, and Deborah Kolb, in a *Harvard Business Review* article (September 2013), stated that "People become leaders by internalizing a leadership identity. Internalizing a sense of oneself as a leader is an iterative process. A person asserts leadership by taking purposeful action—that promotes confidence, stepping outside one's comfort zone and gradually becoming a leader." I believe the process that is instrumental to become a leader is also true with becoming a rainmaker. Thinking of yourself as a rainmaker, or "rainmaker in process," leads you toward taking action that strengthens confidence toward achieving your business development goals. It is critical, these authors suggest, to place yourself in as many situations as you can to act "like a rainmaker" so that you can gradually adopt the identity for which you strive. Small successes beget greater levels of success. This is not a "fake it 'til you make it" strategy. Rather, in a phrase similar to the one in the movie *Field of Dreams*, "Believe that you can be a rainmaker and the relationships will come."

Chapter 36

Gender Differences

Many unproductive walls separate male and female lawyers when it comes to business development, such as "the old boys' network," where client relationships are often born and flourish; women's initiative events at spas, holiday shopping sprees and "women only" cocktail parties; and closed-door chats inside firms where members of the same gender gather. While social psychology perspectives point to people feeling more comfortable with people who are like themselves, this tendency must be busted in order to thrive in the "new normal" business climate, where all relationships rule. For business development to flourish, collaboration must occur, especially collaboration among individuals possessing different strengths, approaches to relationships, access to different networks, expertise, etc.

While there is much to share about how "gender intelligence" (a term used by Barbara Annis and Keith Merron in their book *Gender Intelligence*) can positively impact all avenues of law firm profitability, cultures and structures, in this section I will focus only on how this concept impacts relationships. Before moving ahead, however, I must state an important premise: when I talk about differences between women and men, I speak in generalities that exist along a continuum of variability. The descriptions I discuss may not fit for you or they may correspond only slightly to you. You may have learned to utilize features ascribed to both genders (good for you!). The following is based on a great deal of highly scientific research. I hope you will consider employing it in a way that makes best sense to you.

Now let's dive in. Given different brain structures and biochemical attributes, men and women tend to develop relationships differently. Here are some important proclivities:

1. Men tend to focus on only one attribute of a relationship, such as business, over a short period of time; women tend to focus on multiple aspects of a relationship that develop over the long term.

Individual Liabilities—men may look to close business before a relationship is "ripe" and have little patience for a relationship to evolve over the long term; women may focus on so many aspects of a relationship that they may not pick up clues about available business opportunities.

As a Team—the long term and the short term, close focus and broad focus all receive attention. Each gender can encourage the other to maintain an awareness of domains that may be missed by the other.

2. During conversations, men tend to focus primarily on the overt content of the discussion; women tune in to subtle, nonverbal nuances of a speaker such as voice inflection that may cue excitement or displeasure, eye rolling that indicates skepticism, sighs that may hint at boredom, body posture that may state "I want to know more" or "This conversation is going well," etc.

Individual Liabilities—men may miss important messages that are conveyed "between the lines"; women may be over-attentive to mannerisms and miss a core message.

As a Team—men and women can compare perceptions about a conversation and together decide the best next-step approach.

3. When devising a strategy, men tend to focus primarily on the goal; women tend to focus on the bigger picture and the broad context of multiple aspects occurring at the time.

Individual Liabilities—men may fail to take important influencing factors into account when devising a business strategy; women may be so distracted by "what ifs" that taking action may be delayed too long and strategies may become overcomplicated.

As a Team—a thorough analysis of a marketplace sector can occur that integrates multiple factors as well as a rigorous pursuit of a goal.

4. Men's approach toward a goal tends to be individualistic, rigorous and competitive, where they may focus on their own gains; women's approach toward a goal tends to be team-oriented, contemplative and collaborative.

Individual Liabilities—men may miss the add-ons that can be contributed by others such as knowledge, relationships and skills. They also must manage their competitive drive so that they do not come across negatively to colleagues and clients; women's "we" focus may preclude them from having their specific contributions recognized (this can hinder obtaining due financial credit); involving a lot of people in an effort may take a great deal of time, thus sacrificing efficiency.

As a Team—men and women working together can find a "happy medium" between the individual focus and team focus; men can keep the agenda moving ahead, and women can make sure that input is gathered from teammates.

5. Men's communication styles tend to be data- and fact-driven; they tend to engage in very focused business conversations and are usually not personal and emotional. Women's communication style tends to focus on personal aspects of a relationship; they look for commonalities with the person with whom they are speaking and attempt to elicit sharing from the other party.

Individual Liabilities—men may miss discussing topics that could deepen and expand a relationship; women may miss delving into areas in which they could ultimately conduct business.

As a Team—relationships can be developed more expansively.

Fostering effective gender collaboration requires awareness, recognition and acceptance of differences and patience for all involved. All parties must fight temptations to judge the other gender's style as "wrong" and seek ways to leverage the strengths provided by all. A lot of conversation is needed—usually not a strength of men—and objective (not personalizing) acknowledgement of times when one person's style is not effective—not usually a strength of women. Yet with commitment to making the collaboration work, men and women can blend their strengths into becoming a powerful business development team.

I see the collaboration between the genders as essential for making rain. Begin by inviting together a few colleagues of both genders whom you trust. I recommend that the group read and share reactions to a book that enumerates gender differences (such as *Gender Intelligence* by Barbara Annis and Keith Merron or *Leadership and the Sexes* by Michael Gurian with Barbara Annis). Next, create a strategy that has two focuses: 1) a business development direction (such as we have discussed throughout this book); 2) a process to monitor the way the group is working together with specific attention to making sure that the differences of each person are being utilized, included and respected.

Good Luck. If you have the courage to begin such a process, you are ahead of most of your peers.

Reviewing and Concluding

I can't believe we are done. I have covered a huge amount of material and hope that you have found at least one idea that you want to grab and run with. There are several points that I want to repeat to keep them fresh in your mind.

1. You've read everything and you are ready to GO. Great. Remember that action happens in a three-step sequence:

    WHAT do you want to accomplish?

    WHO can help you get there?

    HOW do you connect and build relationships with your WHOs?

    If you are excited and want to call some people with whom you have connections right away (a HOW), go ahead and have fun doing it. Then *please* return to the WHAT so that all of your actions serve your goals and occur within a well-thought-through strategy.

2. Keep in mind the success equation:

    Rainmaking requires possessing a *constantly growing* WHOs List AND *consistently providing value* to your WHOs.

3. There is no ONE right way or PERFECT way to develop relationships and business. Success occurs YOUR way. Use your intuition when connecting. Do what feels right in a given situation or with a specific person. This allows you to be authentic. Authenticity, integrity and caring sustain relationships. When you use those elements as guides, you will be fostering strong connections even when you are outside of your comfort zone.

4. Success is most powerfully acquired when you leverage YOU:

    - Strengths
    - Values
    - Personality

- Comfort zone
- Work habits
- Likes and dislikes
- Goals

Spend time refreshing your knowledge of these and other aspects of yourself. They are foundational to advancement. We all change over time—that's a given. Get to know yourself at *this* point in time to form a strong base for moving toward creating great things!

5. You are not alone. If you want/need inspiration, guidance, resources, support, gather people you trust around you. Let them know what you are doing. Ask for what you need. Reach out to people who may have knowledge that you don't have. Don't be afraid to be vulnerable—you are learning; we have all been there and hopefully always will be. Allow yourself to enjoy the process of learning from your successes and failures.

6. Do everything you can to take action NO MATTER WHAT, no matter how small the undertaking. Every task leads you to goals that are important to you. Keep your precious goals in mind and stretch forward.

Of course, I don't personally know each and every one of you who is reading this book, but in whatever way is possible, I am thinking about you and cheering for you. I dearly want you to reach your dreams. Please contact me if I can be helpful. Consider me to be a part of your support circle. Believe me, I know firsthand how daunting the quest of developing business can feel, and often, can be. As you work through each step, experiment, gain confidence and achieve even the smallest of wins, I would love to hear about it. Being in this together will allow us all to succeed. Thank you for honoring me by reading this book. I look forward to hearing from you, learning from you and connecting with you. You can contact me at Karen@ThresholdAdvisors.com.

Bibliography

Collins, Jim, *Good to Great: Why Some Companies Make the Leap ... and Others Don't,* HarperCollins Publishers Inc.: New York (2001).

Burg, Bob, and Mann, John David, *The Go-Giver: A Little Story About a Powerful Business Ideal,* The Penguin Group (USA) Inc.: New York (2007).

Saujani, Reshma, *Women Who Don't Wait in Line: Break the Mold, Lead the Way,* Houghton Mifflin Harcourt Publishing Company: New York (2013).

Robinette, Judy, *How to Be a Power Connector: The 5+50+100 Rule for Turning Your Business Network into Profits,* McGraw-Hill Education (2014).

Sobel, Andrew, *All for One: 10 Strategies for Building Trusted Client Partnerships,* John Wiley & Sons, Inc.: (2009).

Klauser, Henriette Anne, *Write It Down, Make It Happen: Knowing What You Want— And Getting It!,* Simon & Schuster, Inc.: New York (2000).

Seligman, Martin E. P., *Authentic Happiness: Using the New Positive Psychology to Re-alize Your Potential for Lasting Fulfillment,* Simon & Schuster, Inc.: New York (2002).

Kay, Katty, & Shipman, Claire, *The Confidence Code: The Science and Art of Self-Assur-ance—What Women Should Know,* HarperCollins: New York (2014).

Annis, Barbara, & Merron, Keith, *Gender Intelligence: Breakthrough Strategies for In-creasing Diversity and Improving Your Bottom Line,* HarperCollins: New York (2014).

Passarella, Gina, and Needles, Zack, "GCs to Law Firms: Employ Caution When Cross-Selling," *The Legal Intelligencer,* March 25, 2014.

Ibarra, Herminia, Ely, Robin, and Kolb, Deborah, "Women Rising: The Unseen Barri-ers," *Harvard Business Review,* September 2013.

Appendix A

Threshold Advisors™ WHOs List

Company	Contacts	Notes	Action Plan/ Needs/Outcome	Action
ABC Retail	John Smith–GC	New to ABC Retail, alum from firm, son plays basketball	Meet at INTA Conference 5/12 to discuss Internet branding issues	Asked for checklist about Great branding—sent on 5/15—follow up 5/22

For an electronic copy of the WHOs List, go to www.DauntingToDOable.com/Tools.

Appendix B

Threshold Advisors™ Business Development Blueprint

NAME _____ **DATE** _____

Q. Summarize your business development **focus** going forward?

A.

Q. What do you see as the "hot topic" or topics in your **practice area today** and over the near term?

A.

Q. What do you see as the "hot topic" or topics in your **niche or major area of industry** focus today and in the near term?

A.

Q. What do you see as your most significant **challenges** to your business development success over the next twelve months?

A.

Q. What do you see as the most significant **opportunities** for your business development success over the next twelve months?

A.

Q. What is your plan for maintaining the business development momentum from the past several months?

A.

Q What resources (not time) could best support your business efforts?

A.

Q. By this time next year I will have ...

A.

For an electronic copy of the Blueprint, go to www.DauntingToDOable.com/Tools.

About the Author

Karen is the person lawyers call when their business development efforts, or any part of their career for that matter, feels daunting. She is also the person who leaders in the legal profession contact when they want a new way to think about "tired" topics, business models and ways of practicing. Her warm, engaging manner is sprinkled with optimism, curiosity and a true commitment to wanting to help people and organizations succeed. Sometimes provocative and challenging, other times nurturing and supportive, she blends psychologist, coach, teacher, leader, thinker, strategist, personal trainer, professional, colleague and friend into one wise woman.

Formal credentials can be found at www.thresholdadvisors.com. What's most important, is that, while not a lawyer, Karen has developed a depth of experience and breadth of knowledge to understand the challenges and opportunities faced by lawyers. She continuously studies the legal marketplace as well as the constantly evolving models of practicing law.

Working with Karen, either coaching or consulting, is a highly individualize pursuit. All programs and services are specifically designed to fit each person, law firm and legal department—no cookie-cutters with Karen. If you have exhausted all that you know and success, advancement and real progress seem unattainable, talk to Karen and explore a potential direction and plan.

Contact Karen at Karen@ThresholdAdvisors.com to get inspired, learn, explore and collaborate.

What else should you know about Karen? That she is a devoted mother, daughter, partner, sister, dog lover, friend and colleague. She lives her dream, on the beach in Westport, Connecticut where she grew up. Baking desserts and making homemade ice cream are particular passions and she is known as quite a wedding producer.

Above all, Karen is a passionate connector, a practicer of "finding the yes" and "the and," and she believes strongly in the power of people helping each other succeed.

Index

exercises
    on confidence, 186–187
    on fear/failure, 177–178
experimenting
    interactions, 48, 61
    with intermediate goals, 154–155
    with LinkedIn, 115–116
    at networking events, 96–97
    with niches, 39–40, 42

F

face-to-face contact, 105–106
    See also networking events
failure
    as an attitude, 182
    fear of, 177–179
family
    as a resource, 143–144
    as contacts, 31*fig*
feedback
    asking for, 56, 105, 167, 174, 178
    critical, 182
Feedly, 121
fishing metaphor, 89–90
five "I"s of Business Development, 5–7, 37
Flipboard, 121
follow-up strategies
    after networking events, 97–99
    and debriefing, 98
FORD (Family, Occupation, Recreation and Dreams), 52–53, 62, 72, 98, 108, 133
framing, concept of, 174–175
frequently asked questions
    on marketing, 36
    on origination credits, 37–38
    on sub-niches, 37
friends, as contacts, 30, 31*fig*, 32, 42, 66

HOWs
    and authenticity, 46
    and behavior, 107
    connecting with clients, 148–149
    and curiosity, 47
    defined, 23
    and giving, 45–47
    and opportunities, 47
    and the Relationship Marathon™, 107–108
    and relationships, 71–73, 75–78, 147
    without WHOs, 23
    See also conversations; networking events; WHATs; WHOs

I
ideals, 5, 6
identity and success, 189–190
immediate goals, 153–154, 156
impacts, 5, 6
in-person connection. *See* face-to-face contact
income, 5, 7
independence, 5–6, 37
indulgences, 5, 6–7
industries
    and learning about clients, 76–77, 77*fig*
    recording information about, 77*fig*
    researching, 85–87
industry niches
    hot topics in, 127–128, 130
    learning about, 77, 77*fig*
    and networking events, 91
    and WHOs Lists, 85
    See also needs; niches
inner rolodex techniques, 83–84
inspiration, from business development diaries, 135
intermediate goals, 154–155, 156

N

O

offering
  and awareness of needs, 58*fig*, 67
  defined, 65
  See also The Ask
"old-boy's network", 112, 191
old school approach to networking, 112–113
one degree of separation, 32, 38
one-on-one meetings, 106
  See also face-to-face contact
opportunity
  identifying, 128–129
  and WHOs Lists, 47
origination credits, 15, 37–38, 66

P

past and current clients
  phone conversations with, 104
  relationships with, 28–30
  and your WHOs List, 41–42
perfectionism, 173–175
personal and professional networks
  challenges with, 31–32
  people on the list, 31*fig*
  talking about business with, 79–81
  WHO's List and, 30–33, 42, 45
  See also networking
personal dreams
  Sally's story, 4–5
  See also FORD (Family, Occupation, Recreation and Dreams)
pessimism, 171–172
  See also perfectionism
phone calls. *See* telephone calls
preparation for networking events, 90–92
"pulling" vs. "pushing" relationships, 12, 46, 49–51

relationship development
    and collaboration, 85–86
    and conversations, 55–58
    and face-to-face contact, 105–106
    and follow-up strategies, 98–99
    and giving, 75, 102
    and HOWs, 71–73, 75–78, 147
    inside the firm, 71–73
    over the telephone, 104–105
    priorities, 58*fig*, 66–70
    process of, 50–51
    "pushing" vs. "pulling", 12, 46, 49–51
    and rainmaking, 13–14, 55–58, 99
    through e-mail, 102–104
    See also business development; conversations
relationship managers, assistants as, 140
Relationship Marathon™, 107–109
relationships
    assessing, 101–102
    and authenticity, 50–51
    and business development strategy, 23
    developing, 50–51
    inside the firm, 25–28, 71–73
    with past and current clients, 28–30
    personal and professional networks, 30–33
    "pushing" vs. "pulling", 12, 46, 49–51
    and WHOs Lists, 10, 24
    See also conversations
repositioning yourself, questions about, 166
reputation, 71
research
    with colleagues, 141–143
    and the firm librarian, 140–141
research assistants, 144
resilience, 181–183
resources, 87, 129, 139–144, 161–162
Robinette, Judy (*How To Be A Power Connector*), 57

Made in the USA
San Bernardino, CA
04 March 2016